THE QUICK CHRISTIAN REFERENCE

EVERY BIBLE CHAPTER SUMMARIZED

Joshua Morrison

ISBN: 978-1-961619-63-0

Dedication

I wrote this book for everyone starting or expanding their understanding of the Bible. As a student of Liberty University, I often struggled to find the scripture I needed to support my research papers. My hope is that the next generation of students can use this book to narrow their search.

Acknowledgment

I want to thank my wife and kids and the rest of my family and friends for always listening to my "version" of the Bible. I especially want to thank my Christian role models when I was just starting out: Barry Moll, Chris Mesa, Amy Alexander, and Margret Fields.

About the Author

Joshua Morrison is a native New Hampshire resident. He joined the Army after 9/11 and retired in Granbury, TX. He has been married to his wife, Jennifer, since 2005, and they have three beautiful children, four dogs, and three cats. He is a graduate of Liberty University with a Master of Arts in Human Services.

Table of Contents

Dedication iii

Acknowledgment iv

About the Author v

The Old Testament 1

Genesis 4

Exodus 6

Leviticus 9

Numbers 11

Deuteronomy 14

Joshua 16

Judges 18

Ruth 20

1 Samuel 23

1 Kings 29

2 Kings 32

1 Chronicles 35

2 Chronicles 37

Ezra 39

Nehemiah 41

Esther 44

Job 47

Psalms 49
Proverbs 52
Ecclesiastes 54
Song of Songs 56
Isaiah 58
Jeremiah 60
Lamentations 62
Ezekiel 64
Daniel 66
Hosea 68
Joel 70
Amos 72
Obadiah 74
Jonah 76
Micah 78
Nahum 80
Habakkuk 82
Zephaniah 84
Haggai 86
Zechariah 88
Malachi 90

The New Testament 92
Matthew 94
Mark 96
Luke 99

John 102
Acts 104
Romans..107
1 Corinthians 109
2 Corinthians 111
Galatians..113
Ephesians..115
Philippians 117
Colossians..119
1 Thessalonians 121
2 Thessalonians 123
1 Timothy..125
2 Timothy..127
Titus 129
Philemon 131
Hebrews..133
James..135
1 Peter..137
2 Peter..139
1 John 141
2 John 143
3 John 143
4 John 145
Jude..147
Revelation 149
The Apocrypha..151

Tobit 153
Judith 155
Wisdom 157
Sirach 159
Baruch 161
1 Maccabees 163
2 Maccabees 165

Dead Sea Scrolls 167

This book was written to familiarize oneself with the Bible before taking the plunge and reading one's chosen Bible version from start to finish. Each chapter consists of a summary less than two pages in length.

The Old Testament

The Old Testament, also known as the Hebrew Bible, is a sacred text in Judaism and an important religious document for Christians. It consists of various books written over centuries and encompasses diverse genres such as historical narratives, poetry, wisdom literature, and prophecy.

The Old Testament begins with the book of Genesis, which describes the creation of the world and the origins of humanity. It introduces figures like Adam and Eve, Noah, and Abraham, who become the fathers of the Hebrew people through a covenant with God. The story continues with Abraham's descendants, including Isaac, Jacob, and Joseph, leading to the Israelites' migration to Egypt.

The book of Exodus recounts the Israelites' liberation from slavery in Egypt under the leadership of Moses. They experience miraculous events like the Ten Plagues and the parting of the Red Sea. Moses receives the Ten Commandments and leads the Israelites through the wilderness, eventually reaching the borders of the Promised Land.

Following Exodus, the books of Leviticus, Numbers, and Deuteronomy establish laws, rituals, and ethical principles for the Israelites. These books contain detailed instructions on worship, sacrifices, and social conduct, aiming to create a holy and just community.

The Israelites' conquest of the Promised Land is chronicled in the book of Joshua. The subsequent period is marked by the rule of various judges who led the Israelites during times of crisis. The book of Ruth tells the story of a Moabite woman who becomes an ancestor of King David, establishing the lineage of the future kings of Israel.

The books of Samuel, Kings, and Chronicles cover the period of the monarchy in Israel. Saul became the first king, followed by David, who unified the kingdom and established Jerusalem as its capital. David's son, Solomon, constructed the First Temple, which became the center of worship.

However, the United Kingdom eventually splits into two: Israel in the north and Judah in the south. The prophets emerged as prominent figures during this time, delivering messages of warning and hope. Eventually, both kingdoms are conquered: Israel falls to the Assyrians, while Judah is exiled to Babylon.

During the exile, the books of the prophets convey messages of comfort and restoration. After the exile, some Israelites returned to rebuild Jerusalem and the Second Temple. The books of Ezra and Nehemiah chronicle these events and the reestablishment of Jewish life in the land.

The Old Testament concludes with the writings of the prophets, such as Isaiah, Jeremiah, and Ezekiel. These books contain prophecies of future events, promises of a Messiah, and visions of a restored and righteous society.

In summary, the Old Testament spans the creation of the world, the history of the Israelites, the establishment of laws and rituals, the rise and fall of the monarchy, the exile and return, and the words of the prophets. It is a complex and rich collection of texts that explores themes of faith, covenant, justice, and the human-divine relationship.

Genesis

"Genesis 1:1 – In the beginning, God created the heavens and the earth."

The Book of Genesis is the first book of the Hebrew Bible and the Christian Old Testament. It serves as an introduction to the biblical narrative, providing an account of the creation of the world, the origin of humanity, and the early history of humanity's relationship with God. Here is a summary of Genesis:

In the beginning, God created the heavens and the Earth. He speaks the universe into existence of over six days, forming light, land, seas, vegetation, celestial bodies, fish, birds, animals, and finally, humans. The pinnacle of His creation is Adam and Eve, the first man and woman, whom He places in the Garden of Eden.

God gives Adam and Eve dominion over all creation but commands them not to eat from the Tree of the Knowledge of good and evil. However, the serpent tempted them, and told them to eat from the forbidden tree, resulting in their expulsion from Eden and the introduction of sin and death into the world.

As humanity grows, sin spreads, and the earth becomes corrupt. God decides to flood the earth to rid it of evil but saves Noah and his family, instructing Noah to build an ark and bring animals of every kind aboard. After the flood, God made a covenant with Noah, promising never to destroy the earth by water again and establishing the rainbow as a sign of His covenant.

The descendants of Noah multiply and fill the earth. However, the people rebel against God and attempt to build the Tower of Babel, a monument to their greatness. In response, God confuses their language and scatters them across the earth, creating different nations and languages.

The narrative then focuses on the life of Abraham, whom God chooses to bless and make into a great nation. God promises Abraham that he will have numerous descendants, and all the families of the Earth will be blessed through him. God tests Abraham's faith when God commands him to sacrifice his son Isaac, but at the last moment, God provides a ram for the offering.

Abraham's descendants continue through his son Isaac and grandson Jacob, who was later renamed Israel. Jacob has twelve sons, who become the fathers of the twelve tribes of Israel. One of his sons, Joseph's brothers sell him into slavery, but he rises to prominence in Egypt. Through a series of events, Joseph becomes a powerful ruler and saves his family from a famine, leading them to settle in Egypt.

The book concludes with the death of Joseph, marking the end of the patriarchal era and setting the stage for the events of Exodus.

In summary, the Book of Genesis presents the creation of the world, the fall of humanity, the judgment of the flood, the scattering of nations, and the beginnings of God's chosen people through the lives of the patriarchs, particularly Abraham, Isaac, Jacob, and Joseph. It lays the foundation for the rest of the biblical narrative, setting the stage for God's plan of redemption and salvation.

Exodus

"Exodus 20:2 – I am the LORD your God, who brought you out of the land of Egypt, out of the house of slavery."

Exodus is a biblical book that narrates the story of the Israelites' liberation from slavery in Egypt and their subsequent journey to the Promised Land. The book divides into several sections, each highlighting different events and themes.

The story begins with the Israelites' oppression under Pharaoh, who feared their growing population. God calls upon Moses, an Israelite raised in Pharaoh's palace, to be the deliverer of his people. After witnessing the suffering of his brethren, Moses confronts Pharaoh, demanding the release of the Israelites. However, Pharaoh refuses, and a series of plagues are unleashed upon Egypt, displaying God's power. These plagues escalate until the final plague, which kills the firstborn sons of Egypt. The Israelites were instructed to mark their doorposts with the blood of a lamb, which would spare them from the plague's effects.

Following this devastation, Pharaoh finally allowed the Israelites to leave. The Israelites quickly depart, taking with them their livestock and possessions. A pillar of cloud during the day and a pillar of fire guide them at night, both representing God's presence. However, Pharaoh changed his mind and pursued the Israelites with his army. Trapped between the Red Sea and the approaching army, the Israelites fearfully cry out to God. In a miraculous event, Moses stretches out his staff, and the waters of the sea part, allowing the

Israelites to cross on dry land. Once they safely reach the other side, the waters close in, drowning Pharaoh and his army.

The Israelites continue their journey through the wilderness, but they face numerous challenges. They grapple with scarcity of food and water, leading to their reliance on God's providence. God provides manna, a miraculous bread-like substance, and water from a rock to sustain them. As they travel, the Israelites encounter the Amalekites, a hostile nation. Moses intercedes, and with the help of his companions, Joshua and Hur, the Israelites are victorious.

At Mount Sinai, Moses ascended the mountain to receive the Ten Commandments from God. During his absence, the Israelites grow impatient and create a golden calf to worship. Angered by their idolatry, Moses breaks the stone tablets and confronts the people. After a period of repentance, Moses received a new set of tablets, and the Israelites begin construction of the Tabernacle, a portable sanctuary where God's presence dwells.

The book concludes with the completion of the Tabernacle, a sign of God's faithfulness and the Israelites' commitment to follow His instructions. The glory of the Lord fills the Tabernacle, signifying His presence among His people.

Exodus is a significant book in the Bible as it outlines the foundational story of the Israelites' liberation and the establishment of their covenant with God. It emphasizes God's deliverance, guidance, and provision for His people, while also highlighting the challenges they faced in their journey toward the Promised Land. The events and themes in Exodus foreshadow future biblical narratives and demonstrate the enduring faithfulness of God throughout history.

Leviticus

"Leviticus 18:4 – You shall follow my rules and keep my statutes and walk in them. I am the LORD your God."

Leviticus is the third book of the Hebrew Bible, part of the Old Testament, and it focuses on the laws and regulations given by God to the Israelites through Moses. The book contains a comprehensive set of instructions covering various aspects of religious, moral, and ceremonial practices for the Israelite community. Here is a summary of Leviticus:

The book begins by describing the procedures for offering sacrifices to God, including burnt offerings, grain offerings, peace offerings, sin offerings, and guilt offerings. These offerings meant to atone for sins and maintain a relationship with God. The priests were assigned specific duties and instructions for conducting these sacrifices.

Leviticus also establishes guidelines for the priesthood, outlining the consecration of Aaron and his sons as the high priest and priests, respectively. The priests were responsible for maintaining the sanctuary, offering sacrifices, and acting as mediators between God and the people. Certain restrictions and regulations were set upon them, including rules about their attire, cleanliness, and behavior.

The book then moves on to discuss various laws and regulations concerning moral conduct and social justice. It covers topics such as sexual morality, prohibiting incest, adultery, and homosexuality. It also addresses issues related to the treatment of slaves, the poor, and foreigners, emphasizing fairness and compassion.

Leviticus dedicates significant attention to the concept of ritual purity and impurity. It outlines rules regarding cleanliness and the avoidance of unclean objects, animals, and bodily discharges. These regulations aimed to maintain the holiness of the Israelite community and reinforce their separation from other nations.

In addition to moral and ceremonial laws, Leviticus contains dietary restrictions, known as the kosher laws. It distinguishes between clean and unclean animals, specifying which animals are acceptable for consumption and how they should be prepared. These dietary laws served to emphasize the Israelites' distinctiveness and their obedience to God's commandments.

The book concludes with a section on blessings and curses, known as the blessings of obedience and the curses of disobedience. It emphasizes the importance of following God's commandments and warns of the consequences of disobedience, including exile and loss of God's favor.

Overall, Leviticus serves as a guidebook for the Israelite community, providing them with a comprehensive set of laws and regulations governing their religious, moral, and social lives. It aims to establish their identity as God's chosen people and emphasizes the significance of holiness, obedience, and adherence to God's commandments. While some of the laws may seem unfamiliar or even outdated today, Leviticus played a crucial role in shaping the religious and cultural practices of the ancient Israelites.

Numbers

"Numbers 23:19 – God is not man, that he should lie, or a son of man, that he should change his mind. Has he said, and will he not do it? Or has he spoken, and will he not fulfill it?"

The Book of Numbers, the fourth book of the Hebrew Bible and the Old Testament, is an account of the Israelites' journey from Mount Sinai to the edge of the Promised Land. It derives its name from the several censuses conducted throughout the book. Here is a summary of the Book of Numbers:

The book begins with the completion of the construction of the Tabernacle, a portable sanctuary where God would dwell among the Israelites. The tribes of Israel organized around the Tabernacle, with their respective leaders and responsibilities established and the Levites appointed to assist the priests in their duties.

A census is conducted, numbering all the able-bodied men above the age of 20. The total comes to around 600,000, forming a formidable army. The Israelites arranged in their tribal formations, and the cloud of God's presence guided them, which led them through the wilderness.

The Israelites encounter various challenges and grumble against Moses and God. They complain about their hardships, reminisce about Egypt, and express discontent with their diet of manna. God responds with both mercy and discipline, providing quail for meat and even sending a plague because of their complaints.

Moses appoints seventy elders to share the burden of leadership. Miriam and Aaron speak against Moses, resulting in Miriam being struck with leprosy. After her healing, the journey continues towards the land of Canaan.

Moses sends twelve spies, one from each tribe, to explore the Promised Land. Ten of them bring back a negative report, instilling fear and doubt among the people. Only Joshua and Caleb express faith in God's promise. Due to their lack of faith, God decrees that the generation of Israelites who doubted would not enter the land, and they wandered in the wilderness for forty years until they perished.

During this period, various laws and regulations were imposed, covering topics such as sacrifices, purity, vows, and the duties of the Levites. The Israelites continued to struggle with obedience and faced consequences for their disobedience. Additionally, a rebellion led by Korah, Dathan, and Abiram challenges Moses and Aaron's authority, resulting in their demise.

As the forty-years came closer to an end, the Israelites prepare for their entry into the Promised Land. Moses delivers a series of speeches, recounting their journey and reminding them of God's faithfulness. He reiterates the importance of obeying God's commands and warns against idolatry and intermarriage with the surrounding nations.

The book concludes with the Israelites poised on the eastern side of the Jordan River, ready to cross into the land God promised to give them. Moses prepares to pass leadership to Joshua and reiterates God's commandments before his death.

In summary, the Book of Numbers provides a narrative of the Israelites' journey from Sinai to the edge of the Promised Land. It recounts their challenges, grumblings, and disobedience, as well as God's faithfulness and discipline. The book emphasizes the importance of faith, obedience, and trust in God's promises, while also establishing laws and regulations for the Israelite community.

Deuteronomy

"Deuteronomy 6:5 – You shall love the LORD your God with all your heart and with all your soul and with all your might."

Deuteronomy is the fifth book of the Hebrew Bible and the Christian Old Testament. It is part of the Torah, which is the foundational text of Judaism. The book is attributed to Moses and primarily consists of his final speeches to the Israelites before they entered the Promised Land.

The name "Deuteronomy" is derived from the Greek words meaning "second law," which reflects its nature as a repetition and elaboration of the laws given in the earlier books of Exodus, Leviticus, and Numbers. It serves as a reminder and reiteration of the covenant between God and the Israelites.

The book begins with Moses recounting the Israelites' journey from Egypt and their encounters with various nations along the way. He emphasizes the importance of their obedience to God's commandments and warns them against idolatry and assimilation with the surrounding nations.

Deuteronomy contains a restatement of the Ten Commandments and expands on various aspects of the law, including social, moral, and religious principles. It emphasizes justice, fairness, and compassion, emphasizing the importance of treating one another with kindness and respect. The laws cover a wide range of topics, including marriage and family, agriculture, warfare, and the administration of justice.

Moses stresses the significance of worshiping only the one true God and warns against the worship of other gods or idols. He emphasizes the need for loyalty and fidelity to God and the consequences that will follow if the Israelites turn away from their faith.

The book also lays out the requirements for the establishment of a just society, including the appointment of judges and the fair treatment of widows, orphans, and foreigners. It places a strong emphasis on social responsibility and caring for the less fortunate members of society.

In addition to the laws, Moses recounts the Israelites' history and their relationship with God. He reminds them of their disobedience and the consequences they faced, including the forty years of wandering in the wilderness. Despite their past failures, Moses encouraged the Israelites to trust in God and remain faithful as they prepared to enter the Promised Land.

Deuteronomy concludes with Moses' final blessings and his appointment of Joshua as his successor. Moses reminds the Israelites of the covenant they have with God and urges them to choose life by following His commandments.

Overall, Deuteronomy serves as a reminder of God's faithfulness, the importance of obedience, and the blessings that come from following His laws. It lays the foundation for the Israelites' future as they settle in the land promised to them and reaffirms their identity as God's chosen people.

Joshua

"Joshua 1:9 – Have I not commanded you? Be strong and courageous. Do not be frightened, and do not be dismayed, for the LORD your God is with you wherever you go."

The Book of Joshua is the sixth book of the Hebrew Bible and the Old Testament, providing an account of the Israelites' conquest and settlement of the Promised Land under the leadership of Joshua, Moses' successor. It encompasses a significant period in Israelite history, beginning with the crossing of the Jordan River and concluding with the establishment of the tribes in their allotted territories.

After Moses' death, Joshua assumed leadership and received divine instructions to lead the Israelites across the Jordan River into Canaan. God assures Joshua of his presence and commands him to be strong and courageous. The Israelites follow Joshua's leadership and miraculously cross the Jordan on dry ground.

Once in Canaan, the Israelites embarked on a series of military campaigns to conquer the land. The city of Jericho is the first target, and its walls miraculously collapse after the Israelites march around it for seven days, blow their trumpets, and shout. The Israelites then capture and destroy Ai, but suffer a temporary setback due to disobedience. They resolve the issue and regain victory, continuing their conquest.

As the Israelites advance, they enter into alliances with the Gibeonites, a neighboring Canaanite tribe. However, they soon discover that the Gibeonites had deceived them, posing as a distant people to avoid destruction. Despite the oath made to spare them, Joshua honors the alliance but reduces the Gibeonites to servitude.

Joshua led the Israelite forces in several military campaigns against various Canaanite kings, achieving significant victories. The sun stands still at Gibeon, prolonging daylight, and aiding the Israelites in their battle against their enemies. The southern and northern regions of Canaan witnessed the Israelite conquest, as Joshua captured numerous cities and kings. The book provides a detailed account of the territorial division among the twelve tribes of Israel, guided by the casting of lots.

The book emphasizes the importance of obedience to God's commands. Joshua renews the covenant between the Israelites and God, urging them to remain faithful and avoid idolatry. The Israelites are reminded of God's faithfulness throughout their history and the need to serve Him alone.

In summary, the Book of Joshua recounts the military campaigns and conquests of the Israelites as they settled in the Promised Land under Joshua's leadership. It highlights divine intervention, miraculous victories, and the fulfillment of God's promises. The book also emphasizes the importance of obedience and faithfulness to God, reminding the Israelites of their covenant and the consequences of straying from it.

Judges

"Judges 21:25 – In those days there was no king in Israel. Everyone did what was right in his own eyes."

The Book of Judges is a historical account found in the Old Testament of the Bible. It provides a narrative of the Israelites' journey from the conquest of the Promised Land to the establishment of the monarchy. Judges covers a period of Israel's history marked by cycles of disobedience, oppression, repentance, and deliverance.

The book begins after the death of Joshua, who had led the Israelites in conquering the land of Canaan. With Joshua gone, the Israelites failed to completely drive out the remaining Canaanite inhabitants. As a result, the Israelites find themselves surrounded by idolatry and pagan practices, which lead them astray from their covenant with God.

The pattern established in Judges involves the Israelites turning away from God, serving foreign gods, and facing the consequences of their actions. God responds by allowing neighboring nations, such as the Moabites, Philistines, and Midianites, to oppress them. In their distress, the Israelites cry out to God, who raises leaders known as judges to deliver them.

These judges, chosen by God, serve as military and spiritual leaders for the Israelites. The book highlights various judges, including Othniel, Ehud, Deborah, Gideon, Jephthah, and Samson. Each judge arises in response to the Israelites' cry for help and plays a crucial role in delivering the people from their oppressors.

Despite their flaws, the judges serve as instruments of God's deliverance. Through miraculous victories and acts of bravery, they led the Israelites to triumph over their enemies. However, as time passes, the people often fall back into sin and idolatry, repeating the cycle of disobedience and oppression.

One prominent figure in Judges is Samson, known for his extraordinary strength. God blesses Samson with incredible physical power, but he struggles with personal weaknesses and a lack of self-control. His story is a cautionary tale of the consequences of succumbing to temptation and failing to fulfill God's purpose.

The Book of Judges concludes with a period marked by moral chaos and anarchy. The Israelites become increasingly corrupt, and the book ends with the haunting phrase, "In those days, Israel had no king; everyone did as they saw fit." This sets the stage for the establishment of the monarchy, as the Israelites seek a more stable form of governance.

Overall, the Book of Judges portrays a cycle of disobedience, oppression, repentance, and deliverance. It reveals the Israelites' struggle to remain faithful to God's covenant and their repeated failure to fully obey Him. The judges serve as imperfect but essential instruments in God's plan to bring salvation and redemption to His people.

Ruth

"Ruth 1:16 – But Ruth said, "Do not urge me to leave you or to return from following you. For where you go I will go, and where you lodge I will lodge. Your people shall be my people, and your God my God."

The Book of Ruth is a narrative found in the Hebrew Bible, specifically in the Ketuvim (Writings) section. Set during the time of the Judges in ancient Israel, the book tells a touching story of loyalty, love, and redemption. It revolves around the lives of four main characters: Naomi, Ruth, Boaz, and Orpah.

The story begins in the land of Moab, where a famine drives an Israelite family, consisting of Elimelech, his wife Naomi, and their two sons, to seek refuge. While in Moab, tragedy strikes, and Elimelech passes away, leaving Naomi a widow. Her sons, Mahlon and Chilion, marry Moabite women named Orpah and Ruth.

Over ten years, both sons also die, leaving Naomi alone with her daughters-in-law. Distraught and with no hope for the future, Naomi decides to return to her homeland, Bethlehem, as she hears that the famine has ended. She urges her daughters-in-law to stay in Moab and find new husbands, but Ruth refuses to leave her side. Orpah reluctantly bids farewell to Naomi and returns to her people, while Ruth remains steadfastly loyal to her mother-in-law.

Upon arriving in Bethlehem, Ruth takes it upon herself to support Naomi by gleaning in the fields owned by Boaz, a wealthy and honorable man. Boaz notices Ruth's hard work and kindness and is impressed by her loyalty to Naomi. He offers her protection and allows her to gather grain from his fields. Naomi recognizes the significance of Boaz's favor and encourages Ruth to pursue him as a potential redeemer—a man who could marry her and carry on the family lineage.

Following Naomi's advice, Ruth visits Boaz at night and expresses her desire for him to fulfill the role of a redeemer. Boaz commends Ruth for her virtuous character and promises to handle the matter. However, another potential redeemer has a closer relative claim to Ruth's deceased husband's inheritance. Boaz confronts this relative and presents him with the opportunity, but the relative declines, allowing Boaz to step in as the redeemer.

Boaz and Ruth marry, and their union brings hope and joy to Naomi's life. Ruth gives birth to a son named Obed, who becomes the grandfather of King David—an important figure in Israel's history. The book concludes by emphasizing Ruth's remarkable loyalty, her integration into the Israelite community, and the redemption and restoration she experiences.

The Book of Ruth highlights several key themes, including loyalty, selflessness, the value of virtuous character, and the providence of God. It demonstrates that acts of kindness, faithfulness, and integrity can lead to unexpected blessings and can be used by God to accomplish His purposes.

Overall, the Book of Ruth portrays a beautiful story of love, commitment, and divine providence, highlighting how the choices of individuals can have a significant impact on their lives and the lives of those around them.

1 Samuel

"1 Samuel 16:7 – But the Lord said to Samuel, "Do not look on his appearance or on the height of his stature, because I have rejected him. For the LORD sees not as man sees: man looks on the outward appearance, but the LORD looks on the heart."

The book of 1 Samuel is a narrative that recounts the transition of Israel from a period of judges to the establishment of a monarchy. It encompasses the life of the prophet Samuel, the rise and fall of King Saul, and the anointing of David as the future king of Israel.

The story begins with the birth of Samuel, who is dedicated to the service of God by his mother, Hannah. Samuel grows up under the guidance of the high priest Eli, and he becomes a prophet who communicates with God. During this time, the Israelites faced various challenges, including the Philistine oppression.

As the Israelites demand a king to lead them, despite Samuel's warnings about the potential negative consequences, God instructs Samuel to anoint Saul, a young and tall Benjamite, as the first king of Israel. Saul initially displays signs of humility and success in battles against the Philistines, but his disobedience to God's commands leads to his downfall.

Saul's disobedience begins when he offers a sacrifice instead of waiting for Samuel, who was supposed to perform the ritual. This act displeases God, and Samuel informs Saul that his kingship will be taken away from him. Saul's disobedience further escalates when he fails to destroy the Amalekites, sparing their king and valuable possessions against God's explicit command.

In the meantime, God directs Samuel to anoint a new king from the house of Jesse. Samuel discovers David, the youngest son of Jesse, who possesses a heart devoted to God. David is anointed in secret, and the Spirit of the Lord comes upon him.

David's reputation grows when he defeats the Philistine giant Goliath with a single stone from his sling. This victory earns him favor with King Saul, but Saul becomes increasingly jealous of David's popularity. Saul attempts to kill David multiple times, forcing David to flee and live as a fugitive.

During his time on the run, David gathers a group of loyal followers, including Samuel, and they live in the wilderness. Saul, driven by his paranoia, pursues David relentlessly, but David refrains from harming Saul, respecting his anointed position.

Eventually, Saul is killed in battle against the Philistines, and David mourns his death. The elders of Israel recognize David's leadership qualities and anointed him as the king of Judah. However, Saul's son, Ish-bosheth, is made king over the other tribes of Israel.

A civil war ensues between the house of David and the house of Saul, and David emerges victorious. He became the undisputed king of Israel and established his capital in Jerusalem, bringing the Ark of the Covenant to the city. Despite facing various challenges, David's reign marks a significant period of strength and expansion for the Israelites.

In summary, the book of 1 Samuel tells the story of the transition from the period of judges to the establishment of a monarchy in Israel. It highlights the rise and fall of King Saul and the anointing of David, who became a central figure in Israel's history. The book emphasizes the importance of obedience to God and the consequences of disobedience.

2- Samuel

"2 Samuel 7:16 – And your house and your kingdom shall be made sure forever before me. Your throne shall be established forever."

The book of 2 Samuel is a part of the Old Testament in the Bible and continues the account of Israel's monarchy. It depicts King David's reign, triumphs, and struggles. Here is a summary of the book in 500 words or less:

2 Samuel opens with the news of King Saul's death, and David mourns for his fallen predecessor and his close friend Jonathan. David, whom God anointed through the prophet Samuel, becomes the new king of Israel. He begins his reign in Hebron, where he is initially recognized as the king of the tribe of Judah.

As David consolidates his power, he faces opposition from Saul's remaining loyalists. However, his military victories and diplomatic skills gradually unite the nation under his rule. The city of Jerusalem becomes the capital of Israel, and David brings the Ark of the Covenant there, symbolizing God's presence among His people.

David desires to build a temple for God, but God reveals to him through the prophet Nathan that his son will build the temple instead. Both, triumphs and failures mark David's reign. He defeats the Philistines, expands Israel's borders, and establishes a mighty kingdom. However, his personal life is marred by instances of moral failure.

One such instance is his affair with Bathsheba, the wife of Uriah the Hittite, one of David's loyal warriors. When Bathsheba becomes pregnant, David orchestrates Uriah's death in battle to cover up the scandal. God sends Nathan to confront David, and the king repents, but he faces the consequences of his actions. The child born from his illicit relationship dies, and David's family experiences internal strife and tragedy.

Amidst these challenges, David's military successes continue. He defeats neighboring nations and establishes Israel as a dominant force in the region. The book also includes accounts of David's mighty men, a group of loyal warriors who perform valiant acts in battle.

In the latter part of 2 Samuel, a series of conflicts arise within David's own family. His son Absalom rebels against him, seeking to seize the throne. Absalom's rebellion gains momentum, and David is forced to flee Jerusalem. A civil war ensues, resulting in a battle in which Absalom is killed. David mourns the loss of his son, causing his victorious troops to feel conflicted.

After the rebellion, David regains control of the kingdom, but further challenges plague his rule. A famine strikes the land, and David seeks to atone for Saul's previous mistreatment of the Gibeonites by handing over Saul's descendants for execution. David also faces a final threat from a Philistine giant, but his warriors rescue him.

The book concludes with a hymn of praise from David, expressing gratitude to God for His faithfulness and deliverance. David's reign ends, and his son Solomon succeeds him as king.

In summary, the Book of 2 Samuel portrays the rise and reign of King David, a man after God's own heart, highlighting his victories, moral failures, and the challenges he faced as the king of Israel. It explores themes of repentance, loyalty, and the consequences of sin while also emphasizing God's sovereignty and faithfulness throughout Israel's tumultuous history.

1 Kings

"1 Kings 3:9 – Give your servant therefore an understanding mind to govern your people, that I may discern between good and evil, for who is able to govern this your great people?"

The Book of 1 Kings is a historical and prophetic account found in the Old Testament of the Bible. It is the eleventh book of the Hebrew Bible and the Christian Old Testament. Here is a summary of the key events and themes found in 1 Kings:

The Book of 1 Kings begins with the final days of King David, the great king of Israel. As he approaches his death, David appoints his son Solomon as his successor. Solomon ascends to the throne and seeks wisdom from God, which he is granted in abundance. He demonstrates his wisdom through various judgements, including the famous case of two women claiming to be the mother of a child.

Solomon's reign is marked by peace, prosperity, and the construction of the magnificent Temple in Jerusalem. He forms alliances through marriage with other nations, but his many wives lead him astray, causing him to worship foreign gods. This displeases God, and as a result, Solomon faces consequences, including the division of the kingdom.

After Solomon's death, his son Rehoboam becomes the king of Judah, while Jeroboam, a former servant of Solomon, leads the ten northern tribes in rebellion, forming the kingdom of Israel. This division creates ongoing tension between the two kingdoms throughout the book.

The Book of 1 Kings introduces a succession of kings in both Judah and Israel, highlighting their varying degrees of faithfulness to God. The kings of Israel, in particular, became notorious for their idolatry and disobedience. Prophets, such as Elijah and Elisha, rise during this time to confront and challenge the wickedness of the kings and the people.

Elijah, a prominent prophet, confronts the evil King Ahab and his wife Jezebel, who promote the worship of the false God Baal. Through various miracles and confrontations, Elijah demonstrates the power and supremacy of the true God. He challenges the prophets of Baal to a dramatic showdown on Mount Carmel, where God vindicates Elijah by sending fire from heaven.

After Elijah, his disciple Elisha continued the prophetic ministry and performed numerous miracles, including healing the sick, multiplying food, and even raising the dead. Elisha also advises kings and plays a crucial role in the events of the time.

Throughout the book, the kings of Israel and Judah experience victories, defeats, and conflicts with neighboring nations such as Aram (Syria) and Assyria. The Book of 1 Kings concludes with the death of Ahab, the rise of his son Ahaziah in Israel, and Jehoshaphat becoming the king of Judah.

In summary, the Book of 1 Kings traces the reigns of Solomon, Rehoboam, and subsequent kings of Israel and Judah. It explores the themes of wisdom, idolatry, obedience, faithfulness, and the role of prophets in confronting evil and calling the people back to God. It serves as a historical account of the divided kingdom and the challenges faced by its leaders, ultimately pointing to the need for wholehearted devotion to the true God.

2 Kings

"2 Kings 13:23 – But the LORD was gracious to them and had compassion on them, and he turned toward them, because of his covenant with Abraham, Isaac, and Jacob, and would not destroy them, nor has he cast them from his presence until now."

The Book of 2 Kings is a part of the Old Testament of the Bible and continues the narrative of the Israelite monarchy from the Book of 1 Kings. It encompasses a period of around 250 years, from the reign of King Ahaziah of Judah to the fall of Jerusalem and the Babylonian exile.

The book begins with the death of King Ahaziah of Israel and the ascension of his brother Jehoram to the throne. Jehoram's reign is marked by wickedness and idolatry, leading to losing territories to neighboring nations. The prophet Elisha played a prominent role during this time, performing miracles and guiding the kings of Israel and Judah.

After Jehoram, Jehu rises to power through events orchestrated by God and the prophet Elisha. Jehu carries out God's judgement upon the wicked house of Ahab, killing both King Jehoram of Israel and King Ahaziah of Judah. Jehu also executes Jezebel, Ahab's wife, putting an end to her influence. However, Jehu himself falls into idolatry and fails to follow God's commandments fully.

The subsequent kings of Israel continued in the pattern of wickedness and idol worship. God raises prophets like Elisha and

Elisha's successor, Jehonadab, to deliver warnings and rebukes to the kings and people. During this time, Israel faced invasions and defeats at the hands of the Arameans, Assyrians, and other neighboring nations.

In Judah, the southern kingdom, a few righteous kings emerge, including Jehoshaphat and his son Jehoram. However, most kings follow the idolatrous nations' ways and lead the people astray. Prophets like Elijah, Isaiah, and Micah speak out against these sinful practices and foretell the judgement that will befall the nation.

The fall of Samaria, the capital of Israel, to the Assyrians marks a significant turning point. The Assyrians exiled the Israelites, scattering them throughout their empire. The northern kingdom of Israel ceases to exist, and the ten tribes are lost to history.

In Judah, King Hezekiah institutes reforms and restores the worship of Yahweh. He removed the idols and repaired the temple in Jerusalem. He also experiences a miraculous deliverance from the Assyrian king Sennacherib, who fails to conquer Jerusalem.

However, after Hezekiah, the kingdom of Judah deteriorated rapidly. King Manasseh reintroduces idol worship and engages in wickedness, provoking God's anger. The subsequent kings did not bring about any lasting reforms, and the nation's decline continued.

The book concludes with the fall of Jerusalem to the Babylonians, led by King Nebuchadnezzar. The city is destroyed, and its inhabitants are taken into captivity. The book ends on a note of sorrow and devastation as the once-glorious kingdom of Judah comes to a tragic end.

In summary, the Book of 2 Kings portrays a narrative of the Israelite monarchy's decline, characterized by idolatry, disobedience, and God's judgement. It highlights the role of prophets and the consequences of forsaking God's commandments. Ultimately, the book serves as a warning about the dangers of turning away from God and the tragic consequences that can result from such actions.

1 Chronicles

"1 Chronicles 29:11 – Yours, O LORD, is the greatness and the power and the glory and the victory and the majesty, for all that is in the heavens and in the earth is yours. Yours is the kingdom, O LORD, and you are exalted as head above all."

The Book of 1 Chronicles is an Old Testament book that serves as a historical record of the genealogies, reigns, and deeds of the Israelite kings and priests from the time of Adam to the exile of the Babylonians. It focuses on the lineage of the Israelite tribes, particularly the tribe of Judah, and highlights the importance of worship, obedience, and the Davidic dynasty.

The book begins with a genealogical account tracing the ancestry of the Israelites from Adam to the twelve tribes of Israel. It emphasizes the significance of the tribe of Judah, which eventually led to the birth of King David, whom God chose to be the king of Israel. The genealogy establishes the legitimacy and divine purpose of the Davidic monarchy.

1 Chronicles then delves into David's reign and the establishment of Jerusalem as the religious and political center of the nation. The book highlights the role of the Levites and priests in worship and the organization of the temple services. It emphasizes the importance of following God's commandments, offering sacrifices, and maintaining proper worship practices.

David's desire to build a permanent temple for God becomes a central theme in 1 Chronicles. However, God instructs David through the prophet Nathan that his son, Solomon, would be the one to fulfill this task. David then gathers resources and prepares the plans for the temple, which Solomon ultimately builds during his reign.

The book also provides an account of David's numerous battles and victories, as well as his preparations for passing on the kingdom to his son Solomon. It documents the organization of the Levitical priesthood, the appointment of various officials, and the allocation of duties for the temple service.

1 Chronicles concludes with David's death and Solomon's succession as the king of Israel. The narrative highlights Solomon's wisdom, wealth, and the grandeur of the temple he built in Jerusalem. The book ends by recording the genealogies of the remaining tribes and the Levites, emphasizing the continuity of God's chosen people.

Overall, the Book of 1 Chronicles reinforces the Davidic lineage and the importance of worship and obedience to God's commands. It highlights the establishment of Jerusalem as the religious center and the role of the Levites and priests in maintaining the worship practices of the Israelites. The book also emphasizes the significance of the temple and its role in the Israelite society.

2 Chronicles

"2 Chronicles 16:9 – For the eyes of the LORD run to and fro throughout the whole earth, to give strong support to those whose heart is blameless toward him. You have done foolishly in this, for from now on you will have wars."

The Book of 2 Chronicles is a part of the Old Testament in the Bible and serves as a historical account of the kings of Israel and Judah, primarily focusing on the kingdom of Judah. It is a continuation of the Book of 1 Chronicles and covers the period from the reign of King Solomon to the Babylonian exile.

The book begins with the reign of Solomon, who succeeds his father, David, as the king of Israel. Solomon built the magnificent temple in Jerusalem and experienced a period of peace and prosperity. However, as he ages, he turns away from God and allows foreign influences to corrupt the kingdom.

After Solomon's death, his son Rehoboam became the king, but his rule was marked by division and rebellion. The northern tribes of Israel separated from the southern kingdom of Judah, leading to two separate kingdoms: Israel in the north and Judah in the south.

Throughout 2 Chronicles, the author evaluates the kings of both kingdoms, focusing on their faithfulness to God and adherence to His commandments. Many kings of Israel and Judah deviated from God's ways, leading to periods of idolatry and moral decline. However, some kings, such as Asa, Jehoshaphat, Joash, Hezekiah, and

Josiah, are commended for their efforts to restore the worship of God and lead their people in righteousness.

The book highlights several key events and reforms during the reigns of these faithful kings. For example, King Asa removes idols and restores the altar of the Lord. King Jehoshaphat institutes religious reforms and appoints judges throughout the land. King Joash repairs the temple and reinstitutes temple worship. King Hezekiah destroys idolatrous altars and reinstitutes the Passover. King Josiah discovers the Book of the Law in the temple and initiates a comprehensive reform, destroying idols and restoring proper worship.

However, despite the efforts of these righteous kings, the majority of the kings and the people continue to stray from God's commandments. Prophets are sent to warn the people of the consequences of their disobedience, but their messages often go unheeded. As a result, God allows foreign nations, such as the Assyrians and Babylonians, to conquer and exile the Israelites.

The book concludes with the Babylonian exile and the destruction of Jerusalem and the temple. However, it also provides a glimmer of hope by ending with the decree of King Cyrus of Persia, allowing the Israelites to return to their land and rebuild the temple.

In summary, the Book of 2 Chronicles recounts the history of the kings of Israel and Judah, emphasizing their obedience or disobedience to God. It illustrates the consequences of straying from God's ways and the potential for restoration and redemption through repentance and adherence to His commandments.

Ezra

"Ezra 7:10 – For Ezra had set his heart to study the Law of the LORD, and to do it and to teach his statutes and rules in Israel."

The Book of Ezra is a historical account found in the Hebrew Bible, specifically in the Old Testament. It provides insights into the events and challenges faced by the Jewish people during their return from exile in Babylon to Jerusalem and the subsequent restoration of their religious practices and community.

The book is divided into two main parts: the first part focuses on the exiles' return under Zerubbabel's leadership, while the second part centers around the priest and scribe Ezra.

In the first part, King Cyrus of Persia issues a decree allowing the Jewish exiles to return to Jerusalem and rebuild the temple destroyed by the Babylonians. Zerubbabel, a descendant of the Davidic line, leads a group of exiles back to Jerusalem. They face opposition from neighboring peoples but manage to lay the foundation of the new temple. However, the construction was halted due to various challenges and political changes.

The narrative then shifts to the second part of the book, where Ezra, a priest and scribe, arrives in Jerusalem during the reign of King Artaxerxes of Persia. Ezra's mission is to enforce the observance of the Law of Moses among the returned exiles. He discovers that some Jews have intermarried with non-Israelite peoples, which goes against the Law. Ezra is deeply troubled by this and urges the people to repent and separate themselves from their foreign wives.

The people respond to Ezra's message, and a gathering is held where they confess their sins and pledge to obey the Law. Ezra plays a significant role in instructing the people on the Law and ensuring its proper observance. He leads a religious reform, restoring the priesthood and the temple worship.

In the later part of the book, Ezra learns about the continued issue of intermarriage and takes further action to address it. He leads a second assembly where the people publicly confess their sins and commit to sending away their foreign wives. The book concludes with a list of those guilty of intermarriage and required to separate from their spouses.

Overall, the Book of Ezra highlights the challenges faced by the Jewish people during their return from exile and emphasizes the importance of obeying the Law of Moses. It showcases the efforts of Zerubbabel and Ezra in rebuilding the temple and reestablishing the community's religious life. The book provides historical context and sheds light on the significance of the restoration period in Jewish history, marking the beginning of a renewed focus on adherence to the Law and the re-establishment of Jerusalem as the center of Jewish worship.

Nehemiah

"Nehemiah 1:6 – let your ear be attentive and your eyes open, to hear the prayer of your servant that I now pray before you day and night for the people of Israel your servants, confessing the sins of the people of Israel, which we have sinned against you. Even I and my father's house have sinned."

The Book of Nehemiah tells the story of a Jewish leader named Nehemiah, who played a crucial role in rebuilding Jerusalem's walls and restoring the Jewish community after their exile in Babylon.

Nehemiah, a cupbearer to the Persian king Artaxerxes, received news about the sad state of Jerusalem's walls and gates. This deeply troubled him, and he sought the king's favor to allow him to return to Jerusalem and undertake the task of rebuilding. Artaxerxes granted Nehemiah's request, providing him with resources and protection.

Upon arriving in Jerusalem, Nehemiah inspected the walls at night and shared his plans with the people. Despite facing opposition from neighboring officials, Nehemiah rallied the Jewish community, assigning them specific sections of the wall to rebuild. They worked tirelessly, each person taking responsibility for their assigned portion. The work progressed rapidly despite ongoing threats from enemies who sought to disrupt the rebuilding efforts.

Nehemiah not only oversaw the physical reconstruction but also addressed internal issues within the Jewish community. He confronted oppression and usury among the wealthy Jews and encouraged them to restore fairness and mercy towards their fellow countrymen. He also tackled the problem of intermarriage with foreign nations, emphasizing the need to maintain the distinctiveness and purity of the Jewish people.

Amidst the rebuilding process, Nehemiah faced numerous challenges. Enemies conspired to attack Jerusalem and plotted to lure Nehemiah away from the city to harm him. However, Nehemiah displayed courage and wisdom, implementing defensive strategies to protect the workers and the city.

In addition to rebuilding the walls, Nehemiah demonstrated a heart for the spiritual restoration of the people. He gathered the people for a public reading of the Law of Moses, renewing their commitment to God and His commandments. This led to a revival and a period of repentance among the Jewish community.

Nehemiah's leadership and determination inspired the people to complete the rebuilding of the walls in a remarkable 52 days. The restored walls not only provided security for the inhabitants but also symbolized the restoration of Jerusalem's strength and identity as the holy city of God.

Throughout the book, Nehemiah exemplifies the qualities of a faithful leader. He relied on prayer and sought God's guidance in all his decisions. He demonstrated perseverance in the face of opposition and inspired unity among the people. Nehemiah's dedication to Jerusalem's physical and spiritual restoration is a powerful example of leadership, faith, and the restoration of a community.

In summary, the Book of Nehemiah recounts the story of a Jewish leader who played a pivotal role in rebuilding Jerusalem's walls. Nehemiah's determination, leadership, and reliance on God successfully restored the city and its people. The book emphasizes the importance of faith, unity, and preserving one's distinct identity in the face of opposition.

Esther

"Esther 4:14 – For if you keep silent at this time, relief and deliverance will rise for the Jews from another place, but you and your father's house will perish. And who knows whether you have not come to the kingdom for such a time as this?"

The Book of Esther is a compelling narrative in the Hebrew Bible, highlighting the events that took place during the reign of King Ahasuerus (Xerxes I) in ancient Persia. It revolves around the life of a Jewish orphan named Esther, who becomes queen and plays a crucial role in saving her people from annihilation.

The story begins with King Ahasuerus organizing a grand feast, displaying his wealth and power. During the festivities, he orders Queen Vashti to appear before his guests, but she refuses, leading to her dethronement. A nationwide beauty pageant is held in search of a new queen, and Esther, a beautiful young woman of Jewish descent, is chosen as the king's new bride. However, her Jewish identity is kept secret under the counsel of her cousin Mordecai.

Stationed at the palace gates, Mordecai uncovers a plot to assassinate the king, which he promptly reports to Esther. The conspiracy is thwarted, and Mordecai's loyalty is recorded in the royal chronicles. Meanwhile, the king elevates a powerful noble named Haman, who becomes Mordecai's adversary.

Haman is deeply offended when Mordecai refuses to bow down to him, and his pride is further wounded when he discovers Mordecai's

Jewish heritage. Driven by vengeance, Haman plots to annihilate all Jews in the Persian Empire. Casting lots (Purim in Hebrew), he determines the date for their destruction. Upon learning of this imminent danger, the Jewish people mourned and fasted.

Mordecai urges Esther to intercede with the king on behalf of her people. Initially hesitant, as approaching the king uninvited could result in death, Esther musters courage and decides to risk her life for her people. She invites the king and Haman to a series of banquets where she cleverly reveals her Jewish identity and exposes Haman's wicked plan.

Enraged by Haman's treachery, the king orders his execution on the gallows Haman had prepared for Mordecai. However, the decree to destroy the Jews remains in effect, as royal edicts cannot be reversed. Instead, the king grants Mordecai and Esther the authority to issue a counter-decree allowing the Jews to defend themselves against their enemies.

The day arrives when the Jews are set to be attacked, but they successfully defend themselves throughout the empire. The Jews emerge victorious, and the day of their deliverance is celebrated as the festival of Purim. Mordecai, now in a position of power, institutes the annual observance of Purim, ensuring that future generations would remember the events and continue to celebrate their salvation.

The Book of Esther emphasizes several significant themes, including the sovereignty of God, courage in the face of adversity, and the preservation of the Jewish people. It serves as a reminder that even in times of great peril, hope and deliverance can come from unexpected sources. Esther's bravery and selflessness are inspiring examples for readers, demonstrating the impact of one person's actions in shaping history and safeguarding a community.

Job

"Job 1:21 – And he said, "Naked I came from my mother's womb, and naked shall I return. The LORD gave, and the LORD has taken away; blessed be the name of the LORD."

The Book of Job is a profound and thought-provoking piece of ancient wisdom literature found in the Old Testament of the Bible. It explores the age-old question of human suffering and the nature of God's justice. The narrative revolves around a man named Job, who is described as a righteous and prosperous individual.

The story begins by introducing Job as a man of great wealth, with a loving family and a strong faith in God. However, one day, God permits Satan to test Job's faith by taking away his possessions, causing the death of his children, and afflicting him with painful sores. Job's life is suddenly plunged into profound suffering, and he is left to grapple with the meaning of his pain.

Job's friends, Eliphaz, Bildad, and Zophar, visit him to offer comfort but engage in a philosophical debate with him. They adhere to the conventional wisdom of the time, arguing that suffering is a direct consequence of sin. They insist Job must have committed some hidden wrongdoing to deserve his suffering. However, Job vehemently defends his innocence and questions the justice of his afflictions. He yearns for an audience with God to plead his case.

Amid his anguish, Job passionately expresses his despair, challenging God's justice and demanding an explanation for his suffering. God finally responds to Job's plea by appearing in a whirlwind. Instead of providing direct answers, God asks Job a series of rhetorical questions that highlight the limitations of human understanding. God's response emphasizes His unfathomable power and wisdom, reminding Job of the vastness of creation and the complexity of the universe.

Overwhelmed by the divine encounter, Job acknowledges his limited understanding and humbles himself before God. He realizes that he cannot fully comprehend the mysteries of life and accepts that God's ways are beyond human comprehension. Job repents of his audacity and confesses his faith in God's sovereignty.

Ultimately, God restores Job's fortunes twofold, blessing him with even greater prosperity than before. God rebukes Job's friends, who had accused him, for their misguided judgements. This serves as a lesson that human wisdom and reasoning can fall short when grappling with the deep questions of suffering and divine justice.

The Book of Job offers profound insights into the nature of suffering, the mystery of God's ways, and the limits of human understanding. It challenges simplistic notions of cause and effect, emphasizing the complexities of life and the need for humility in the face of adversity. Ultimately, Job's story encourages readers to trust in God's wisdom and to find solace in surrendering to His divine plan, even amid profound suffering.

Psalms

"Psalm 103:1 – Bless the LORD, O my soul, and all that is within me, bless his holy name!"

The Book of Psalms is a collection of ancient Hebrew poetry and songs attributed to various authors, including King David. Comprising 150 chapters, it is the largest book in the Bible and holds significant religious and literary importance. While it is challenging to summarize such a rich and diverse book in a limited space, here is a brief overview of the key themes and content in Psalms.

The Psalms cover a wide range of human experiences and emotions, expressing joy, praise, thanksgiving, lament, confession, and supplication. They provide a means for individuals and the community to communicate with God, offering prayers and songs in various situations and circumstances.

The book can be divided into several categories. The first and most prominent category is the psalms of praise and thanksgiving, which extol the greatness of God, His creation, and His acts of deliverance. These psalms express gratitude and awe, encouraging believers to worship and thank God for His goodness and faithfulness.

Another significant category is the psalms of lament and supplication. These poems convey the heartfelt cries of individuals or the community in times of trouble, pain, or persecution. The authors pour out their anguish, pleading for God's help, justice, and deliverance. They express their trust in God's faithfulness and seek His mercy and intervention.

The book also contains psalms of wisdom and instruction, imparting moral and spiritual guidance. These psalms reflect on the Law of God, the righteous way of living, and the consequences of both righteous and wicked behavior. They provide wisdom and insight into God's ways, inviting readers to follow His path and live with integrity.

The Book of Psalms also includes historical psalms that recount Israel's history and God's faithfulness to His people. These psalms remind the community of God's covenant promises, His mighty acts of deliverance, and the importance of remembering and passing on their shared heritage.

Throughout the book, there is a strong emphasis on the attributes and character of God. He is portrayed as the creator, sustainer, and sovereign ruler of the universe. His steadfast love, faithfulness, justice, and mercy are celebrated. The Psalms also acknowledge God's role as a refuge, protector, and source of hope and strength.

The Book of Psalms resonates with readers because it addresses the human condition in all its complexity. It provides comfort and assurance in times of distress, encouragement, inspiration in times of joy, and a framework for expressing one's deepest emotions and desires to God. It serves as a prayer book and a hymnal, inviting believers to engage in personal and communal worship and reflection.

In summary, the Book of Psalms is a diverse collection of poetry and songs that express the full range of human experiences and emotions concerning God. It is a source of spiritual nourishment, guidance, and inspiration for individuals and communities, encouraging them to seek God's presence, worship Him, and find solace in His unfailing love and faithfulness.

Proverbs

"Proverbs 3:6 – In all your ways acknowledge him, and he will make straight your paths."

The Book of Proverbs, found in the Old Testament of the Bible, is a collection of wise teachings and sayings attributed to King Solomon and other wise men. It offers practical guidance on various aspects of life, including wisdom, morality, relationships, and good governance. Spanning 31 chapters, Proverbs presents a rich tapestry of insights and principles that resonate with readers across generations.

The book begins by stating its purpose: to impart wisdom, discipline, and understanding. It emphasizes the fear of the Lord as the foundation of knowledge, highlighting the importance of seeking divine guidance and living in accordance with God's principles. The fear of the Lord is not paralyzing, but rather a deep reverence and respect for God and His wisdom.

Proverbs consistently emphasizes the pursuit of wisdom as the key to a fruitful and righteous life. It extols the virtues of knowledge, understanding, and discernment. It encourages readers to value wisdom above material wealth, for wisdom leads to sound decision-making and a life of righteousness.

The book contains numerous contrasts and comparisons highlighting the consequences of different choices. It contrasts the way of the righteous, which leads to life and blessing, with the way of the wicked, which leads to destruction and ruin. It warns against the enticements of sinful desires and urges readers to avoid the path of folly and embrace righteousness and integrity.

Proverbs also addresses various practical aspects of life, such as the power of words. It cautions against gossip, slander, and dishonesty, emphasizing the importance of truthful speech and the potential to bring healing or harm with our words. It encourages humility, diligence, and self-control, recognizing their value in personal and professional spheres.

The book emphasizes the significance of relationships, particularly within the family. It offers parenting guidance, highlighting parents' responsibility to instruct their children and the benefits of a disciplined upbringing. It speaks to the importance of friendship, urging readers to choose companions wisely and avoid the company of the wicked. It emphasizes the value of loyalty, trustworthiness, and kindness in relationships.

Proverbs also touches on matters of justice and governance. It promotes fairness, integrity, and equity in leadership, discouraging corruption and oppression. It emphasizes the responsibility of rulers to seek wisdom and exercise righteous judgement.

Throughout the book, Proverbs personifies wisdom as a female figure, calling out to humanity to heed her voice. It urges readers to listen and apply the teachings, promising that those who find wisdom will find life, favor, and honor.

In summary, the book of Proverbs is a treasure trove of practical wisdom, offering guidance on various topics. It encourages readers to seek wisdom, live righteously, and make choices that lead to a blessed and fulfilling life. It serves as a timeless guide, reminding us of the importance of seeking divine wisdom in our daily lives.

Ecclesiastes

"Ecclesiastes 12:13 – The end of the matter; all has been heard. Fear God and keep his commandments, for this is the whole duty of man."

The Book of Ecclesiastes, attributed to King Solomon, is a profound exploration of the meaning of life and the pursuit of wisdom. It is a poetic and philosophical work that reflects on the human condition, the inevitability of death, and the fleeting nature of worldly pursuits. Ecclesiastes challenges conventional wisdom and offers insights into the pursuit of true happiness and fulfillment.

The book begins with the famous proclamation, "Vanity of vanities, all is vanity!" This phrase sets the tone for the entire book, emphasizing the emptiness and transitory nature of human endeavors. Solomon, known for his wealth and wisdom, reflects on his own experiences and examines the futility of pursuing material wealth, pleasure, and knowledge. He observes that all these things ultimately fail to bring lasting satisfaction and are like chasing after the wind.

Throughout Ecclesiastes, Solomon examines various aspects of life, including work, pleasure, wisdom, and time. He recognizes the toil and hardships associated with human labor, noting that no matter how much one achieves or accumulates, it will eventually be left behind for others. He also explores the pursuit of pleasure and finds it ultimately unsatisfying, as it only provides temporary happiness and cannot fill the void within.

Solomon reflects on the limitations of human wisdom, recognizing that even the wisest and most knowledgeable individuals cannot fully comprehend the mysteries of life and death. He acknowledges the unpredictability and injustices of the world, observing that both the righteous and the wicked face the same fate and that death comes to all, regardless of their status or achievements.

Amid his reflections, Solomon finds some solace in enjoying simple pleasures and acknowledging God's sovereignty. He encourages his readers to find contentment in their daily lives, to appreciate the small blessings, and to honor God in their actions. He emphasizes the importance of living with integrity and embracing the uncertainty of life, knowing that God holds the ultimate judgement.

The book concludes with a call to fear God and keep His commandments. Solomon reminds his readers that everyone will be held accountable for their actions and that there will be a time for judgement. He encourages a life lived in reverence to God, for it is in this relationship that true meaning and fulfillment can be found.

In summary, the Book of Ecclesiastes is a profound meditation on the fleeting nature of life and the search for meaning. It challenges conventional wisdom and offers insights into the emptiness of worldly pursuits. Solomon's reflections led him to acknowledge the limitations of human wisdom and find solace in enjoying simple pleasures and a reverent relationship with God. Ultimately, Ecclesiastes encourages readers to embrace the uncertainty of life and seek true fulfillment in a life lived with integrity and in awe of the divine.

Song of Songs

"Song of Solomon 8:6 – Set me as a seal upon your heart, as a seal upon your arm, for love is strong as death, jealousy is fierce as the grave. Its flashes are flashes of fire, the very flame of the LORD."

The Song of Songs, also known as the Song of Solomon, is a poetic and lyrical book found in the Old Testament of the Bible. Composed by an unknown author, the book consists of a collection of love poems celebrating the beauty of romantic love and desire between a bride and her bridegroom.

The Song of Songs is written as a dialogue between the beloved woman and her lover, expressing their intense affection and longing for one another. The poems are rich in metaphors and vivid imagery, evoking a sense of sensuality and passion. The book explores themes of love, desire, and the power of attraction, capturing the profound emotional and physical connection between two lovers.

The central characters in the Song of Songs are the Shulammite woman, who represents the bride, and the bridegroom, often referred to as the king or the beloved. Their love is portrayed as a strong, irresistible force that draws them together. The woman expresses her admiration for the bridegroom's physical features, such as his eyes, hair, and body. The bridegroom, in turn, praises the woman's beauty and compares her to various natural elements, such as a lily among thorns or a dove in the clefts of a rock.

The book also contains descriptions of their encounters and yearning for one another. They express their desire to be together and their longing to experience the physical and emotional intimacy of their love. The lovers frequently use nature as a metaphor to describe their affection, comparing their love to the beauty of flowers, fruits, and gardens. The imagery highlights the depth and richness of their relationship.

The Song of Songs has an underlying sense of joy and celebration of love. The lovers rejoice in their union and the pleasure they find in one another's presence. Their love is portrayed as a divine gift, something to be cherished and nurtured.

Interpreting the Song of Songs has been a subject of debate throughout history. Some view it as an allegory representing the love between God and His people, while others interpret it as a celebration of human love and sexuality. The book's inclusion in the Bible has sparked various interpretations and discussions among theologians, poets, and scholars.

In summary, the Song of Songs is a collection of poetic love songs that celebrate the beauty of romantic love and desire. It portrays the intense affection and longing between a bride and her bridegroom, using vivid imagery and metaphors to convey the depth of their emotional and physical connection. The book captures the joy and celebration of love, whether understood as a human experience or a divine gift.

Isaiah

"Isaiah 40:31 – but they who wait for the LORD shall renew their strength; they shall mount up with wings like eagles; they shall run and not be weary; they shall walk and not faint."

The Book of Isaiah is a significant prophetic work in the Old Testament of the Bible, attributed to the prophet Isaiah. It is divided into two main sections: chapters 1-39, which focus on the Assyrian period, and chapters 40-66, which address the Babylonian exile and the return of Israel from captivity. The book encompasses many themes, including judgement, salvation, Messianic prophecies, and the restoration of Israel.

In the first section, Isaiah emphasizes the rebellious nature of Israel and its need for repentance. He warns the people of impending judgement due to their idolatry, social injustices, and lack of faithfulness to God's covenant. Despite this message of judgement, Isaiah also provides glimpses of hope and restoration, promising a future Messianic king who will establish justice and righteousness.

In the second section, Isaiah shifts his focus to the Babylonian exile. He consoles the exiled Israelites and offers comfort by proclaiming God's faithfulness and His plan for their restoration. Isaiah speaks of a new exodus, where God will lead His people back to the Promised Land and rebuild Jerusalem. He emphasizes the unique role of Cyrus, the Persian king, as God's instrument for the liberation of Israel.

Throughout the book, Isaiah delivers numerous Messianic prophecies, which anticipate the coming of a Savior who will bring ultimate redemption and establish God's kingdom on earth. These prophecies speak of a "Servant of the Lord" who will suffer on behalf of the people, providing salvation through His sacrificial death. The descriptions of this Servant foreshadow Jesus Christ and His redemptive work.

Isaiah's visions also include glimpses of the future glory of Israel. He envisions a time when all nations will stream to Jerusalem to worship the one true God, and peace and harmony will prevail. The book concludes with a vision of a new heaven and earth where God's people will dwell in everlasting joy and righteousness.

Overall, the book of Isaiah serves as a powerful proclamation of God's sovereignty, justice, and mercy. It highlights the consequences of disobedience, offers hope in times of despair, and points to the ultimate fulfillment of God's promises through the coming of the Messiah. Isaiah's words continue to resonate with believers today, reminding them of God's faithfulness and the assurance of future restoration.

Jeremiah

"Jeremiah 29:13 – You will seek me and find me, when you seek me with all your heart."

The Book of Jeremiah is a prophetic book found in the Old Testament of the Bible. It is attributed to the prophet Jeremiah, who lived during a tumultuous period in ancient Israel's history. The book consists of a collection of prophecies, speeches, and narratives spanning Jeremiah's ministry, which lasted from approximately 626 BC to 586 BC.

Jeremiah's ministry began during the reign of King Josiah, a reformer who sought to restore true worship and righteousness in Israel. However, the people's hearts remained unchanged, and Jeremiah warned them of impending judgement if they did not turn back to God. He called for repentance and fidelity to the covenant with God, emphasizing the need for genuine inner transformation rather than mere external rituals.

Despite his efforts, the people and their leaders continued to drift away from God, practicing idolatry and engaging in social injustices. Jeremiah condemned their idol worship, predicting the destruction of their false gods and warning of the consequences of their actions. He also denounced the prophets who misled the people, speaking falsehoods and offering false hope instead of confronting their sins.

As the political situation in the region became more unstable, Jeremiah faced opposition and persecution. He was accused of treason and faced imprisonment and ridicule. He lamented the destruction that would befall Jerusalem and the temple due to the people's unfaithfulness and lack of repentance. Jeremiah's prophecies of doom were met with resistance and disbelief, but they ultimately came to pass.

The book vividly describes Jerusalem's siege and subsequent fall to the Babylonians in 586 BC. Jeremiah's warnings of captivity and exile were fulfilled as the Babylonians deported many Israelites to Babylon, leaving behind a devastated land. However, even amid this destruction, Jeremiah conveyed messages of hope and restoration, assuring the people that God had not abandoned them altogether. He prophesied a future restoration and a new covenant, promising a time when God would write His laws on their hearts.

Jeremiah's personal struggles and emotions are also evident throughout the book. He experienced loneliness, rejection, and despair but found solace in his relationship with God. His words reflect a deep longing for justice, righteousness, and a genuine relationship with God, even in the face of overwhelming opposition.

In summary, the Book of Jeremiah documents the prophet's ministry during a critical period in Israel's history. It serves as a reminder of the consequences of unfaithfulness and a call to repentance. Despite the impending destruction, Jeremiah's prophecies also offer a glimpse of hope and the promise of restoration. The book emphasizes the importance of an authentic relationship with God and the need for genuine transformation in the hearts of His people.

Lamentations

"Lamentations 3:22 – The steadfast love of the LORD never ceases; his mercies never come to an end;"

The Book of Lamentations is a collection of poetic writings found in the Hebrew Bible. It is traditionally ascribed to the prophet Jeremiah and is believed to have been written after the destruction of Jerusalem by the Babylonians in 586 BCE. The book consists of five chapters, each expressing profound sorrow, grief, and lamentation over Jerusalem's fall and its people's suffering.

The book begins somberly, describing Jerusalem as a once-great city now in ruins. The author mourns the loss of the city's splendor and the devastation that has occurred to its inhabitants. The destruction is seen as the result of God's judgement upon the people for disobedience and unfaithfulness.

The book portrays the people of Jerusalem as experiencing immense suffering and anguish. They are depicted as being in a state of deep mourning, with their hearts heavy and their spirits crushed. The author describes the hardships faced by the people, including hunger, thirst, and the loss of loved ones. The city's walls are destroyed, its temple lies in ruins, and the people are left without hope.

Throughout the book, the author reflects on the reasons behind Jerusalem's destruction. They acknowledge the people's sins and the failure to heed the warnings of the prophets. The author laments the loss of the divine protection that Jerusalem once enjoyed and expresses a deep sense of regret and remorse.

Amidst the overwhelming grief, there are moments of prayer and plea for God's mercy. The author appeals to God's compassion and asks for restoration and redemption. They express hope that God will not abandon them forever and will eventually show mercy to the afflicted.

The book also includes a powerful reflection on the suffering endured by the innocent, particularly the children. The author's heart breaks as they witness the pain and anguish of the young ones caught up in the destruction. The innocence and vulnerability of the children highlight the magnitude of the tragedy and evoke a sense of deep empathy.

In the final chapter, the tone shifts slightly as the author expresses confidence in God's faithfulness. They acknowledge that despite the devastation, God is still sovereign and can bring about restoration. The author calls for repentance and encourages the people to seek God's forgiveness and mercy.

In summary, the Book of Lamentations is a poignant expression of grief and lamentation over the destruction of Jerusalem. It captures the profound sorrow and suffering experienced by the people and reflects on the reasons behind their downfall. Amidst the despair, there are moments of prayer, hope, and a plea for God's mercy. The book serves as a reflection on the consequences of disobedience and a call for repentance and restoration.

Ezekiel

"Ezekiel 36:26 – And I will give you a new heart, and a new spirit I will put within you. And I will remove the heart of stone from your flesh and give you a heart of flesh."

The Book of Ezekiel is a prophetic work found in the Old Testament of the Bible. It consists of 48 chapters and is attributed to the prophet Ezekiel, who lived during the Babylonian exile of the Israelites. God called Ezekiel to be a watchman and messenger to the people of Israel, delivering messages of judgement, warning, and hope.

The book begins with Ezekiel's visionary encounter with the "chariot throne" of God, where he witnesses divine glory and receives his commission as a prophet. He is instructed to speak to the rebellious Israelites, who have turned away from God and embraced idolatry and injustice. Through various symbolic acts and visions, Ezekiel conveys the message of God's impending judgement on Jerusalem and the surrounding nations.

Ezekiel's prophecies against Jerusalem depict the city's impending destruction and the exile of its inhabitants. He uses vivid and dramatic imagery to convey the severity of God's judgement. He denounces the false prophets and leaders who have misled the people and predicts the fall of Jerusalem, which ultimately comes to pass in 586 BCE when the Babylonians destroy the city and exile its people.

Amidst the prophecies of judgement, Ezekiel also offers messages of hope and restoration. He speaks of a future restoration of Israel, where God will gather his people from the nations and bring them back to their land. He envisions a renewed covenant between God and his people, characterized by spiritual renewal, obedience, and the presence of God's Spirit.

Ezekiel's visions include the valley of dry bones, where God breathes life into the dead bones, symbolizing the restoration of Israel. He also envisions a new temple, which represents the dwelling place of God among his people. The detailed description of the temple and its rituals serves as a reminder of the importance of holiness, worship, and obedience.

Throughout the book, Ezekiel emphasizes the accountability of individuals for their own actions. He challenges the idea of collective guilt and emphasizes personal responsibility before God. He underscores the need for repentance and turning away from sin to experience restoration and blessings from God.

In conclusion, the book of Ezekiel is a prophetic work that conveys messages of judgement, warning, and hope. It describes the impending destruction of Jerusalem and the exile of the Israelites but also offers visions of restoration and a renewed covenant between God and his people. Ezekiel's vivid imagery and symbolic acts are powerful reminders of God's justice, sovereignty, and the importance of obedience and repentance.

Daniel

"Daniel 4:35 – all the inhabitants of the earth are accounted as nothing, and he does according to his will among the host of heaven and among the inhabitants of the earth; and none can stay his hand or say to him, "What have you done?"

The Book of Daniel is a significant prophetic and historical book found in the Old Testament of the Bible. It comprises two major sections: the first six chapters consist of narratives about Daniel's life and experiences in the Babylonian Empire. In contrast, the remaining six chapters contain apocalyptic visions and prophecies.

The book opens with Daniel, a young Judean nobleman, and his companions being taken captive by King Nebuchadnezzar of Babylon. They are chosen to be educated in the king's court, where they face the challenge of remaining faithful to their God while living in a foreign land. Daniel and his friends distinguish themselves through their unwavering devotion and gain favor with the king.

In Chapter 2, Nebuchadnezzar has a dream that significantly troubles him. He demands his wise men to interpret the dream, but they are unable to do so. Daniel, guided by God, not only reveals the dream but also its interpretation. This establishes Daniel's reputation as a seer and advisor in the royal court.

The subsequent chapters highlight various encounters and trials Daniel and his friends faced. These include surviving the fiery furnace (Chapter 3) and the lion's den (Chapter 6). Each time, their faith in God remains unshaken, and they emerge unharmed. These stories demonstrate God's power and faithfulness to those who remain steadfast in their devotion.

The second half of the book delves into the prophetic visions Daniel receives. In Chapter 7, he dreams of four beasts representing successive world empires, with the final one symbolizing a future kingdom associated with the end times. Chapter 8 focuses on a vision involving a ram and a goat, foretelling the rise and fall of the Persian and Greek empires.

Chapter 9 contains Daniel's famous prayer of repentance and his plea for the restoration of Jerusalem. In response, the angel Gabriel appears to Daniel and provides a seventy-week prophecy outlining the future events leading up to the Messiah's arrival and subsequent destruction of Jerusalem.

The remaining chapters (10-12) contain highly symbolic and intricate visions of future events. These visions touch upon the rise and fall of various kingdoms, the persecution of the Jewish people, and the ultimate victory of God's kingdom. They provide a glimpse into eschatological events, including the resurrection of the dead and the final judgement.

Overall, the Book of Daniel presents a unique blend of history, prophecy, and apocalyptic literature. It showcases the faithfulness of Daniel and his companions in the face of adversity and their commitment to serving God in a foreign land. It also provides insight into God's sovereignty over the nations and His ultimate plan for the future.

Hosea

"Hosea 6:6 – For I desire steadfast love and not sacrifice, the knowledge of God rather than burnt offerings."

The Book of Hosea is one of the prophetic books found in the Old Testament of the Bible. It is attributed to the prophet Hosea and contains a powerful message of God's love, faithfulness, and the consequences of Israel's disobedience. The book consists of 14 chapters and offers a profound insight into the relationship between God and His people.

Hosea begins by using his personal life as an analogy for God's relationship with Israel. God commands him to marry a woman named Gomer, who represents the unfaithfulness of the Israelites. Gomer repeatedly cheats on Hosea and leaves him, but he continues to love her and eventually brings her back, symbolizing God's enduring love for His people despite their unfaithfulness.

The central theme throughout the book is the spiritual unfaithfulness of Israel and its consequences. God accuses Israel of idolatry, worshiping other gods, and turning away from Him. He laments their unfaithfulness, describing it as spiritual adultery. Hosea warns of the impending judgement and destruction that will come upon Israel as a result of their disobedience.

Despite the message of judgement, the book also emphasizes God's compassion and desire for reconciliation. Hosea speaks of God's longing to restore the relationship with Israel if they would only turn back to Him. He calls on the people to repent and seek God's forgiveness, urging them to forsake their sinful ways and return to the Lord.

Hosea depicts the consequences of Israel's disobedience through vivid imagery and metaphors. He describes their impending destruction as a harvest of judgement and compares it to a reaping whirlwind. The nation will suffer greatly, experiencing famine, warfare, and exile. Yet, despite these hardships, Hosea reminds the people that God's love is steadfast and His desire to restore them remains.

The book concludes with a message of hope. Hosea prophesies a future restoration for Israel, a time when they will return to God and experience His blessings once again. He speaks of God's faithfulness and promises to heal their land, reconciling them to Himself. The restoration will be marked by righteousness, love, and knowledge of God.

In summary, the Book of Hosea presents a powerful message of God's love and faithfulness in the face of Israel's unfaithfulness. It serves as a reminder of the consequences of disobedience and the call to repentance. Despite the impending judgement, the book also offers hope for restoration and a renewed relationship between God and His people.

Joel

"Joel 2:13 – and rend your hearts and not your garments. Return to the Lord your God, for he is gracious and merciful, slow to anger, and abounding in steadfast love; and he relents over disaster."

The Book of Joel is a short but profound prophetic book found in the Old Testament of the Bible. It is attributed to the prophet Joel and provides insight into his message and the events of his time.

The Book of Joel begins with a call to attention, urging the people of Judah to listen and pass on the message to future generations. Joel reveals that a devastating locust invasion has swept across the land, leaving destruction in its wake. This catastrophe serves as a metaphor for a more significant judgement to come.

Joel interprets the locust invasion as a warning from God. He implores the people to repent and return to the Lord, urging them to fast, weep, and mourn as a sign of their genuine remorse. Joel emphasizes that their outward expressions of repentance must be accompanied by inward transformation.

The prophet declares a day of the Lord, a time of divine judgement and reckoning. He describes it as a day of darkness and gloom when the sun, moon, and stars lose their radiance. The day of the Lord is presented as a time of great terror and upheaval when the Lord will intervene in history to judge the wicked and deliver the righteous.

Joel calls for a solemn assembly, urging the people to gather and cry to the Lord for mercy. He assures them that if they genuinely turn to God, He will respond with compassion, forgiveness, and restoration. Joel offers hope amid the impending judgement, promising that God will pour His Spirit on all people, resulting in prophecy, visions, and dreams.

The prophet also addresses the nations that have mistreated Judah. He prophesies against Tyre, Sidon, and Philistia for their acts of violence and exploitation. He warns that God will repay them for their evil deeds.

In the later part of the book, Joel speaks of the restoration and blessings that will follow the judgement. He envisions a time when God will gather His people from all nations and restore their fortunes. The land will be fruitful once again, overflowing with abundance. The Lord's presence will dwell in Zion, and Jerusalem will be holy and secure.

Joel concludes his message by announcing God's judgement on the nations and His dwelling among His people. He declares that God will avenge the blood of His people and bless Judah abundantly. The book ends with a promise of eternal peace and security for God's people.

In summary, the book of Joel communicates a message of warning, repentance, and hope. It emphasizes the need for genuine repentance and turning back to the Lord in times of crisis. While judgement is inevitable, God offers mercy, restoration, and blessings to those who seek Him. The book concludes with the assurance of God's ultimate victory and establishing His eternal kingdom.

Amos

"Amos 5:14 – Seek good, and not evil, that you may live; and so the LORD, the God of hosts, will be with you, as you have said."

The Book of Amos, found in the Old Testament of the Bible, is a prophetic book attributed to the prophet Amos. It consists of nine chapters and provides valuable insights into ancient Israel's social, moral, and religious conditions during the eighth century BCE.

Amos was a shepherd from Tekoa, a small village in Judah. God called him to deliver a message of judgement and warning to the northern kingdom of Israel. Despite being an outsider from the priestly and prophetic circles, Amos fearlessly proclaimed God's word.

The book begins with a series of judgements against Israel's neighboring nations, highlighting their sins and impending punishment. This serves as a backdrop to emphasize that God's judgement is not limited to one particular group but extends to all who engage in injustice and immorality.

Amos then directs his attention towards Israel, delivering a stern rebuke for their social injustices and religious hypocrisy. He condemns the wealthy elites who exploit the poor and neglect the needs of the marginalized. He exposes the rampant corruption in the legal system, where justice is perverted for personal gain. Amos also criticizes the religious rituals and sacrifices that the Israelites perform without true devotion and righteous living. He calls for genuine repentance and a transformation of hearts, urging the people to seek justice and righteousness.

Amos vividly portrays the impending judgement that will befall Israel. He uses vivid imagery, including locusts, fire, and a plumb line, to symbolize the devastation that will come upon the nation due to its unfaithfulness to God's covenant. The prophet emphasizes that no amount of religious rituals or external piety can shield the people from God's judgement if their hearts remain unchanged.

Despite the stern warnings and judgement, Amos offers a glimmer of hope. Amid the impending disaster, he speaks of a future restoration and a remnant that will be saved. He looks forward to the day when justice and righteousness will flow like a river, and God's people will be restored to their land.

In summary, the book of Amos delivers a powerful message of God's judgement against social injustice, religious hypocrisy, and moral corruption. It serves as a call to repentance and transformation, urging the people of Israel to turn back to God and pursue justice and righteousness. Although judgement is imminent, the book also offers hope for restoration and future reconciliation with God. Amos reminds us that genuine faith is not just about religious rituals but is manifested through a life of justice, compassion, and devotion to God.

Obadiah

"Obadiah 1:4 – Though you soar aloft like the eagle, though your nest is set among the stars, from there I will bring you down, declares the LORD."

The Book of Obadiah is the shortest book in the Old Testament of the Bible, consisting of only 21 verses. It is attributed to the prophet Obadiah and contains a prophecy against the nation of Edom. The central theme of the book is divine judgement and retribution.

The book begins with a proclamation from God to the nations, announcing His intention to bring them low and make them small among the nations. The focus then shifts to Edom, a neighboring nation of Judah that descended from Esau, the brother of Jacob. Edom is condemned for its pride and arrogance and its mistreatment of the people of Judah.

Obadiah declares that despite Edom's perceived strength and security, it will be brought down and utterly destroyed. The prophet highlights Edom's complacency and betrayal towards their brother nation, Judah, when they were distressed. Instead of offering support or refuge, Edom took advantage of the situation, looted their cities, and handed over the surviving Israelites to their enemies.

The punishment for Edom's actions is prophesied to be severe. The day of the Lord is depicted as a time of reckoning when the nations face the consequences of their deeds. Edom's wealth and allies will not be able to save them from this divine judgement. The nation will be plundered, its allies will turn against it, and its wise men will be deceived. Edom's destruction will be so complete that there will be no survivors.

The reason for Edom's downfall is attributed to its violence and mistreatment of others. The book of Obadiah emphasizes the principle of divine justice, stating that as Edom had done to others, so it will be done to them. The oppressed will rise against the oppressor, and the wicked will face their deserved punishment.

In contrast to Edom's fate, the book ends with a promise of deliverance for the house of Jacob. Judah will possess the land that once belonged to Edom, and the kingdom will be restored. The people of Israel will return from their exile and inhabit their rightful territories. The ultimate victory and sovereignty belong to God, and His rule will be established over all the earth.

In summary, the book of Obadiah serves as a warning and a message of hope. It condemns the nation of Edom for its pride, betrayal, and mistreatment of others. It prophesies their downfall and emphasizes the principle of divine justice. However, it also promises the restoration of Israel and the establishment of God's kingdom. The book conveys the timeless message that those who oppress and mistreat others will ultimately face the consequences of their actions, while God's justice and redemption will prevail.

Jonah

"Jonah 2:9 – But I with the voice of thanksgiving will sacrifice to you; what I have vowed I will pay. Salvation belongs to the LORD!"

The Book of Jonah is a brief and intriguing narrative found in the Hebrew Bible. It tells the story of Jonah, a prophet who receives a divine command from God to go to the city of Nineveh and warn its inhabitants of their impending destruction due to their wickedness. However, instead of obeying, Jonah attempts to flee from God's presence by boarding a ship bound for Tarshish.

During the voyage, a violent storm arises, threatening to destroy the ship and its crew. Recognizing that Jonah is the cause of their misfortune, the sailors cast lots to determine who is responsible, and the lot falls on Jonah. Realizing the gravity of his actions, Jonah confesses that he is fleeing from God and advises the sailors to throw him into the sea to calm the storm. Reluctantly, the sailors comply and toss Jonah overboard.

As Jonah is thrown into the raging waters, a great fish—often described as a whale—swallows him. Jonah remains in the belly of the fish for three days and three nights, during which he prays to God for deliverance. In response to his plea, God commands the fish to vomit Jonah onto dry land.

Having been given a second chance, Jonah receives the same divine commission to go to Nineveh. This time, he obeys and enters the city, proclaiming that Nineveh will be overthrown in forty days. Surprisingly, the people of Nineveh responded immediately and wholeheartedly to

Jonah's message. They believe in God, declare a fast, and put on sackcloth as a sign of repentance—from the lowest to the highest ranks of society.

Witnessing the people's repentance, God relents from destroying Nineveh and spares the city. This outcome greatly displeases Jonah, who becomes angry with God for showing mercy. He retreats to the city's outskirts, hoping to witness its destruction. God then causes a plant to grow and provide shade for Jonah, but the next day, God sends a worm to destroy the plant, exposing Jonah to the scorching sun.

Overwhelmed by the heat and his anger, Jonah wishes for death. God questions Jonah's anger over the plant's demise, highlighting the inconsistency of his compassion for the plant and lack of concern for the lives of the people in Nineveh. God emphasizes His own compassion for the people of Nineveh, including their many innocent inhabitants and animals. The book concludes with God's rhetorical question, challenging Jonah's self-righteousness and narrow perspective.

The Book of Jonah offers valuable lessons about the inclusiveness of God's mercy, the importance of obedience to divine commands, and the need for humility and compassion. It serves as a reminder that God's concern extends beyond national boundaries and should inspire individuals to reflect on their own attitudes toward mercy and justice.

Micah

"Micah 6:8 – He has told you, O man, what is good; and what does the LORD require of you but to do justice, and to love kindness, and to walk humbly with your God?"

The Book of Micah, found in the Old Testament of the Bible, is a prophetic work attributed to the prophet Micah. The book comprises seven chapters and addresses the social, political, and religious issues prevalent during the eighth century BCE in the kingdoms of Israel and Judah. Here is a summary of the book:

Micah begins by introducing himself and declaring his prophecy against Samaria and Jerusalem, the capitals of Israel and Judah, respectively. He denounces the corruption and injustice prevalent in society, highlighting the oppression of the poor by the powerful. Micah emphasizes that God will judge the nations for their sins.

The prophet then focuses on the rulers, priests, and prophets who exploit their positions for personal gain. He rebukes them for leading the people astray and engaging in dishonest practices. Micah declares that true worship of God requires justice, mercy, and humility rather than mere religious rituals.

Micah foretells the destruction of Samaria and Jerusalem due to their transgressions. He describes the devastation that will befall the cities, as well as the exile and captivity of the people. However, amidst the judgement, Micah offers hope for the future restoration of God's people and the establishment of a righteous kingdom.

The prophet prophecies about the coming Messiah, highlighting Bethlehem as the birthplace of the future ruler who will bring peace and shepherd the people. This messianic prophecy is later referenced in the New Testament, connecting it to the birth of Jesus Christ.

Micah continues by condemning various social injustices prevalent in society, such as dishonesty, violence, and greed. He calls for repentance and transformation, urging the people to seek justice and walk humbly with God.

The book concludes with a powerful reminder of God's faithfulness and compassion. Micah praises God's mercy, forgiveness, and steadfast love. He acknowledges the covenant between God and His people and expresses confidence in God's promise to restore and bless them.

In summary, the Book of Micah is a prophetic work that exposes the sins and injustices of Israel and Judah. It emphasizes the importance of justice, mercy, and humility in worshiping God and highlights the consequences of disobedience. Despite the impending judgement, Micah offers hope for restoration, pointing to the coming Messiah and highlighting God's faithfulness and love for His people. The book serves as a call to repentance and a reminder of God's sovereignty and compassion.

Nahum

"Nahum 1:7 – The LORD is good, a stronghold in the day of trouble; he knows those who take refuge in him."

The Book of Nahum is a prophetic book found in the Old Testament of the Bible. It consists of three chapters and is named after its author, Nahum, a prophet from Elkosh. Written in the seventh century BCE, Nahum's prophecies primarily focus on the city of Nineveh and its impending destruction.

The book begins with Nahum proclaiming God's justice and wrath against Nineveh, the capital of the Assyrian Empire. Nahum describes God as a jealous and avenging God who will not let the guilty go unpunished. He declares that the Lord is slow to anger but will ultimately bring judgement and destruction upon those who oppose Him.

Nahum vividly portrays the might and power of God as he describes the Lord's approach to Nineveh. The mountains quake, the earth trembles, and the seas dry up at His presence. The city's fortifications are futile against the impending judgement of God. Nahum portrays the Lord as a jealous lover, determined to avenge the harm done to His people by the Assyrians.

Nahum recounts the wickedness and brutality of the Assyrians, emphasizing their oppression of other nations and the Israelites. He describes their military might and the terror they instilled in their enemies. Despite their strength, Nahum assures the people that the Assyrians' days are numbered and their empire will soon crumble.

Nahum prophesies the fall of Nineveh in vivid detail. He describes the siege of the city, its gates being opened, and its defenses being breached. He declares that the once-glorious city will become a desolate wasteland filled with mourning and devastation. The destruction will be so complete that no remnant of Nineveh's greatness will remain.

The book concludes with a song of celebration as Nahum rejoices in the downfall of Nineveh. He describes the relief and joy that other nations will experience when they witness the destruction of their oppressor. Nahum affirms that the Lord is good and a stronghold for those who trust in Him in times of trouble. He encourages the people of Judah to observe their solemn feasts and fulfill their vows, for the Assyrians will no longer trouble them.

In summary, the book of Nahum is a prophetic account of God's judgement against the city of Nineveh and the Assyrian Empire. Nahum portrays God as a powerful and just avenger who will bring about the downfall of the wicked. Despite the Assyrians' strength and oppression, Nahum assures the people that their destruction is inevitable and that God will be a refuge for His faithful followers.

Habakkuk

"Habakkuk 3:2 – O LORD, I have heard the report of you, and your work, O LORD, do I fear. In the midst of the years revive it; in the midst of the years make it known; in wrath remember mercy."

The Book of Habakkuk is a relatively short book in the Old Testament of the Bible, consisting of only three chapters. It is categorized as one of the Minor Prophets and is believed to have been written by the prophet Habakkuk around the late 7th century BCE. The book addresses profound questions about God's justice and the existence of evil.

Habakkuk begins by expressing his perplexity to God about the violence and injustice he witnesses in Judah. He questions why God allows wickedness to prevail and why He seems silent in the face of such atrocities. Habakkuk's complaints echo the concerns of many people struggling to reconcile their faith with the suffering and evil they observe in the world.

In response to Habakkuk's inquiries, God reveals His plans to raise the Babylonians to punish Judah for their disobedience. This revelation shocks Habakkuk, as he questions how God could use a nation even more wicked than Judah to bring about justice. He raises concerns about the apparent contradiction between God's holiness and the means by which He achieves His purposes.

God reassures Habakkuk that He will ultimately bring justice. The Babylonians, too, will face judgement for their actions. Habakkuk is instructed to wait patiently for God's appointed time. This waiting period emphasizes the importance of trust and faithfulness, even amid uncertainty.

In the final chapter, Habakkuk acknowledges God's sovereignty and power. He recognizes that God is the source of his strength and expresses his unwavering trust in Him, regardless of the circumstances. Habakkuk's faith is unwavering despite knowing that difficult times lie ahead.

The book concludes with a beautiful prayer and song of praise. Habakkuk declares his commitment to rejoice in God, regardless of the circumstances. He acknowledges God's power to bring salvation and expresses his dependence on Him, even if everything else fails. Habakkuk's prayer serves as a model of faith and demonstrates that true worship and trust in God can transcend circumstances.

In summary, the book of Habakkuk is a dialogue between the prophet and God, wrestling with questions of justice, evil, and God's sovereignty. Habakkuk learns to trust God's ultimate plan, even when it seems perplexing or contradictory. The book emphasizes the importance of faith, patience, and worship, reminding readers that God is in control and will ultimately bring justice and salvation.

Zephaniah

"Zephaniah 3:17 – The LORD your God is in your midst, a mighty one who will save; he will rejoice over you with gladness; he will quiet you by his love; he will exult over you with loud singing."

The Book of Zephaniah, found in the Old Testament of the Bible, is a short prophetic book consisting of three chapters. It is attributed to the prophet Zephaniah, who likely prophesied during the reign of King Josiah of Judah in the late 7th century BCE. Zephaniah's message primarily focuses on the impending judgement and day of the Lord upon the nation of Judah and the surrounding nations due to their sins and unfaithfulness.

The book begins with a proclamation of divine judgement against Judah and Jerusalem. Zephaniah declares that God will utterly destroy everything on the face of the earth and warns the people to repent and seek the Lord before it is too late. He condemns various forms of idolatry, including the worship of foreign gods and engaging in pagan rituals. Zephaniah emphasizes the seriousness of God's impending judgement, stating that it will come swiftly and without mercy.

Zephaniah then turned his attention to the neighboring nations, including Philistia, Moab, Ammon, Cush, and Assyria. He predicts their downfall and destruction, highlighting their pride, violence, and oppression of others. These prophecies serve as a reminder that God's judgement extends beyond Judah to encompass the entire world.

The book takes a hopeful turn in Chapter 2 as Zephaniah urges the people of Judah to gather together and seek righteousness and humility amid judgement. He encourages them to seek the Lord, hoping that they may find shelter and be spared from the coming destruction. Zephaniah envisions a remnant of faithful people who will survive and experience the restoration of God's favor.

The final chapter of Zephaniah describes the future blessings and restoration that God will bestow upon the faithful remnant. Zephaniah foresees a time of joy, where the Lord will remove their punishment, gather the dispersed, and restore their fortunes. God's people will be praised and honored, and their relationship with Him will be renewed.

In summary, the Book of Zephaniah is a prophetic message of impending judgement and hope. Zephaniah denounces the sins of Judah and the surrounding nations, warning of the coming day of the Lord's judgement. However, he also offers hope for a faithful remnant who will seek righteousness and experience God's restoration. The book serves as a call to repentance and a reminder of God's justice and mercy.

Haggai

"Haggai 2:9 – The latter glory of this house shall be greater than the former, says the LORD of hosts. And in this place I will give peace, declares the LORD of hosts."

The Book of Haggai is a short prophetic book in the Old Testament of the Bible, consisting of only two chapters. It was written by the prophet Haggai when the Jewish exiles were returning to Jerusalem after the Babylonian captivity. The book primarily focuses on the rebuilding of the temple in Jerusalem and the spiritual message associated with it.

Haggai begins his prophecy by addressing the people of Judah and their leaders, urging them to consider their ways and the condition of the temple. He rebuked them for their lack of zeal in rebuilding the house of God while they were focused on their own comfortable lives. The prophet reminds them of their hardships and the consequences of neglecting God's house. He emphasizes that their priorities should be aligned with God's will.

The central message of Haggai's prophecy revolves around the importance of rebuilding the temple. He encourages the people to take courage and work on the construction project, assuring them that God is with them. The prophet assures them that although the glory of the second temple might not match the magnificence of the first temple built by Solomon, God's presence will fill it with even greater glory in the future.

Haggai's words inspire Zerubbabel, the governor of Judah, and Joshua, the high priest, along with the people. They respond positively to Haggai's message and begin working on the temple. Despite opposition and discouragement, they persevere with the task, driven by their newfound zeal for the Lord.

The prophet Haggai delivers a message of hope to the people. He promises them that God will bless them and bring prosperity to the land if they remain faithful and obedient. Haggai conveys a vision of a future when God will shake the heavens and the earth, overthrowing the nations and establishing His eternal kingdom.

The people receive Haggai's message, and they complete the rebuilding of the temple within a short span of time. God affirms His presence among them, promising to bless and make them prosper. He declares that Zerubbabel will be His chosen signet ring, symbolizing his position of authority and favor.

The Book of Haggai concludes with a reminder of God's sovereignty and faithfulness to His covenant. The prophet delivers a final message to Zerubbabel, stating that God will overthrow kingdoms and give him a place of honor. This declaration signifies the restoration and the fulfillment of God's promises to His people.

In summary, the book of Haggai emphasizes the importance of prioritizing God's work and aligning one's actions with His will. The prophet calls for the rebuilding of the temple, which symbolizes the spiritual renewal of the people. Haggai's message encourages the people to have faith, persevere, and trust God's faithfulness. The book ends with a promise of future blessings and the establishment of God's eternal kingdom.

Zechariah

"Zechariah 1:3 – Therefore say to them, Thus declares the LORD of hosts: Return to me, says the LORD of hosts, and I will return to you, says the LORD of hosts."

The Book of Zechariah, found in the Old Testament of the Bible, is a prophetic book attributed to the prophet Zechariah. It consists of 14 chapters and provides a message of hope, encouragement, and divine intervention for the people of Israel during a time of restoration and rebuilding.

The book is divided into two main sections. The first section, chapters 1-8, focuses on Zechariah's messages and visions to encourage the Israelites who had returned from the Babylonian exile to rebuild the temple in Jerusalem. Zechariah urges the people to repent and return to the Lord, promising that God will be with them and bless them as they faithfully obey His commands. The prophet emphasizes the importance of true worship, justice, and mercy and warns against hypocrisy and disobedience. Through his visions, Zechariah also foretells the coming of the Messiah and the establishment of God's kingdom.

The second section, chapters 9-14, contains apocalyptic prophecies that go beyond the immediate restoration of Jerusalem and provide a glimpse into the future. Zechariah predicts the triumphal entry of a humble king on a donkey, which is often associated with Jesus' entry into Jerusalem centuries later. The prophet also foresees a time when Jerusalem will be attacked, and the Lord will come to fight for His people, bringing about victory and salvation.

Zechariah's prophecies extend beyond the restoration of Israel and point to a future where God's kingdom will encompass the whole earth. He speaks of a time when all nations will recognize the sovereignty of God and worship Him. The prophet also addresses Israel's spiritual condition, highlighting the shepherd's betrayal and rejection (a reference to Jesus) and the scattering of the flock. However, Zechariah assures that a remnant will be refined and purified through trials and tribulations, and they will recognize and mourn for the One they have pierced.

The book of Zechariah is filled with symbolic imagery, including visions of golden lampstands, flying scrolls, and a measuring line. It emphasizes the importance of spiritual renewal, obedience to God's commands, and the ultimate fulfillment of God's promises. Zechariah's prophecies serve as a reminder of God's faithfulness, His plan for redemption, and the ultimate victory of His kingdom.

In summary, the book of Zechariah contains prophecies and messages of hope and encouragement for the restoration and rebuilding of Jerusalem. It addresses the importance of true worship, justice, and mercy and foretells the coming of the Messiah. Zechariah's visions also extend into the future, pointing to a time when God's kingdom will encompass the whole earth and all nations will worship Him. The book emphasizes the spiritual renewal of Israel and the ultimate fulfillment of God's promises through the refining of a remnant. It serves as a reminder of God's faithfulness, His plan for redemption, and the ultimate victory of His kingdom.

Malachi

"Malachi 3:6 – For I the LORD do not change; therefore you, O children of Jacob, are not consumed."

The Book of Malachi, the last book of the Old Testament in the Bible, consists of a series of prophetic messages delivered by the prophet Malachi. It addresses the spiritual and moral condition of the Israelites during the post-exilic period, highlighting their negligence and unfaithfulness towards God. The book emphasizes the need for repentance, obedience, and the coming of a future messenger who will prepare the way for the Lord.

Malachi begins by declaring God's love for Israel, reminding them of their privileged status as God's chosen people. However, he confronts the Israelites with their failures and points out their lack of honor and reverence towards God. The people offer defiled sacrifices and show little regard for God's name, leading Malachi to rebuke the priests for their negligence and corrupt practices.

The prophet addresses various issues prevalent in society, including intermarriage with foreign women, divorce, and social injustice. He condemns those who divorce their wives unjustly and warns against marrying foreign women who worship foreign gods, as these actions violate the sacred covenant with God.

Malachi rebukes the people for their skepticism and doubts concerning God's justice. The Israelites complained that evildoers prospered while those who served God did not receive their due blessings. In response, Malachi reassures them that God sees their actions and will bring judgement upon the wicked and bless the faithful. He encourages the people to have faith and trust in God's timing and justice.

The book also contains a powerful message about tithes and offerings. The Israelites had neglected their obligation to bring tithes and offerings into the storehouse of the temple, thereby robbing God. Malachi challenges them to test God's faithfulness by bringing the whole tithe and promises that God will abundantly pour blessings upon them.

In the closing chapters, Malachi speaks of a future messenger, often interpreted as John the Baptist, who will prepare the way for the coming of the Lord. This messenger will turn the hearts of the people back to God, signaling a time of redemption and restoration.

The Book of Malachi serves as a call to repentance and obedience. It reveals the consequences of unfaithfulness and warns against complacency in one's relationship with God. The people are urged to return to God wholeheartedly, honor His name, and faithfully obey His commandments. It reminds them of God's faithfulness and His promises of judgement and blessing.

In summary, the Book of Malachi confronts the Israelites with their spiritual and moral failings, urging them to repent, obey, and restore their relationship with God. It emphasizes the importance of faith, integrity, and fidelity in worship, marriage, and social justice. It concludes with the promise of a future messenger who will prepare the way for the coming of the Lord, offering hope for redemption and restoration.

The New Testament

The New Testament is a collection of religious texts that form the second part of the Christian Bible. It comprises 27 books and is divided into four main sections: the Gospels, the Acts of the Apostles, the Epistles (or letters), and the Book of Revelation. This summary aims to provide a concise overview of the key themes and events found in the New Testament.

The New Testament begins with the four Gospels: Matthew, Mark, Luke, and John. They recount the life, teachings, death, and resurrection of Jesus Christ. These accounts highlight Jesus' miracles, parables, and interactions with people from various walks of life. They also emphasize his role as the Messiah, sent by God to bring salvation to humanity through his sacrificial death and subsequent resurrection.

The book of Acts follows the Gospels and focuses on the early Christian community. It describes the actions of the apostles, particularly Peter and Paul, in spreading the message of Jesus throughout the Roman Empire. The Holy Spirit plays a central role, empowering the disciples and enabling the growth of the Church. The Acts of the Apostles also recounts the conversion of Saul (later known as Paul) and his significant contributions to the early Christian movement.

The Epistles consist of letters written by early Christian leaders to various individuals and communities. The Pauline Epistles, authored by the apostle Paul, form the majority of this section. They address theological and practical concerns, offering guidance and encouragement to believers. These letters cover topics such as faith, salvation, Christian living, and the nature of the Church. Other Epistles, such as those written by James, Peter, John, and Jude, provide additional teachings and exhortations to the early Christian communities.

The final book of the New Testament is the Book of Revelation. It is an apocalyptic work attributed to the apostle John. Revelation presents visions and symbolic imagery, unveiling the cosmic conflict between good and evil and the ultimate victory of God. It foretells the return of Jesus, the final judgment, the establishment of God's kingdom, and the renewal of all things.

Throughout the New Testament, recurring themes include love, forgiveness, redemption, and the call to live in accordance with God's teachings. Jesus' central message is to love God and love one's neighbor as oneself. The New Testament also explores the relationship between faith and works, emphasizing the importance of both in the Christian life.

In summary, the New Testament is a collection of books that narrate the life of Jesus, the growth of the early Church, and the teachings of early Christian leaders. It presents the foundational beliefs and values of the Christian faith, offering guidance, inspiration, and hope to believers.

Matthew

"Matthew 6:33 – But seek first the kingdom of God and his righteousness, and all these things will be added to you."

The Book of Matthew is one of the four Gospels in the New Testament of the Bible. It is attributed to the apostle Matthew, also known as Levi, who was a tax collector called by Jesus to become one of His disciples. Matthew's Gospel presents a comprehensive account of Jesus' life, teachings, and ministry, highlighting His role as the long-awaited Messiah and the fulfillment of Old Testament prophecies.

The book begins with a genealogy tracing Jesus' lineage back to Abraham, emphasizing His connection to the covenant promises made to the people of Israel. It then describes the birth of Jesus to the Virgin Mary in Bethlehem and the visit of the Magi who came to worship Him, evoking the fulfillment of prophecies regarding the birth of a Savior.

Matthew focuses on Jesus' teachings, which form the heart of His ministry. The Sermon on the Mount is a central feature. Jesus delivers profound teachings on various topics, including the Beatitudes, love for enemies, prayer, fasting, and the importance of seeking God's kingdom above all else. The Gospel also records many parables and miracles performed by Jesus, illustrating His authority over nature, sickness, and demons.

The Gospel of Matthew highlights Jesus' conflict with the religious leaders of His time. Jesus challenges their legalistic interpretations and presents a higher standard of righteousness, calling for a genuine transformation of the heart rather than mere adherence to external rituals. He exposes their hypocrisy and pronounces judgment upon them while expressing compassion for the marginalized and the outcasts of society.

Matthew devotes a significant portion of his Gospel to the events surrounding Jesus' final week in Jerusalem. It includes His triumphal entry into the city, the cleansing of the temple, intense debates with the Pharisees and Sadducees, and the Last Supper, during which Jesus institutes the sacrament of Communion. The narrative reaches its climax with Jesus' arrest, trial before Pontius Pilate, crucifixion, and resurrection.

The resurrection of Jesus is a pivotal event in Matthew's Gospel. It demonstrates His victory over sin and death, as well as the fulfillment of His promise to be with His followers always. After His resurrection, Jesus commissions His disciples to go and make disciples of all nations, baptizing them in the name of the Father, Son, and Holy Spirit.

In summary, the Book of Matthew presents a comprehensive account of Jesus' life, teachings, and ministry. It highlights His role as the Messiah and the fulfillment of Old Testament prophecies. The Gospel emphasizes Jesus' teachings on righteousness, love, and the kingdom of God, as well as His conflict with religious leaders. It culminates in His crucifixion and resurrection, which provide salvation and hope for all who believe in Him.

Mark

"Mark 10:45 – For even the Son of Man came not to be served but to serve, and to give his life as a ransom for many."

The Book of Mark is one of the four Gospels in the New Testament of the Bible, providing an account of the life and ministry of Jesus Christ. Written by Mark, also known as John Mark, this Gospel is believed to have been composed between 50-70 AD. It presents a concise and fast-paced narrative, emphasizing Jesus' actions and miracles to demonstrate His identity as the Son of God.

The book begins with the ministry of John the Baptist, who prepares the way for Jesus' arrival. John baptizes Jesus, and the Holy Spirit descends upon Him, affirming His divine nature. Immediately after, Jesus is led into the wilderness, where He overcomes Satan's temptations.

Following His time in the wilderness, Jesus begins His public ministry, preaching the good news of the kingdom of God and calling people to repentance. He performs numerous miracles, such as healing the sick, casting out demons, and raising the dead. These extraordinary acts of power and compassion draw both curiosity and opposition from religious authorities.

Mark highlights Jesus' teachings through parables, including the parable of the sower, the mustard seed, and the tenants. These stories convey spiritual truths and challenge listeners to respond with faith and obedience.

Throughout His ministry, Jesus gathers a group of disciples whom He teaches and trains. He selects twelve of them as apostles, whom He sends out to preach, heal, and cast out demons. Jesus shares with them the mysteries of the kingdom of God, revealing that He will suffer, die, and be resurrected.

As Jesus' popularity grows, so does the opposition from religious leaders. They question His authority, challenge His teachings, and plot to kill Him. In the face of this opposition, Jesus continues to heal and teach, revealing His true identity gradually. He asks His disciples, "Who do you say that I am?" and Peter answers, "You are the Christ."

In the final days of Jesus' life, He enters Jerusalem triumphantly, riding on a donkey. This event, known as the Triumphal Entry, signifies His kingship and sets the stage for His ultimate purpose: to offer Himself as a sacrifice for the sins of humanity.

The narrative reaches its climax with the Last Supper, where Jesus institutes the Lord's Supper, predicting His betrayal by one of the disciples. He then goes to the Garden of Gethsemane to pray, agonizing over His impending suffering. Judas, one of the Twelve, betrays Jesus, leading to His arrest.

Jesus endures a series of trials, culminating in His crucifixion. He is mocked, beaten, and nailed to a cross, where He breathes His last breath. At that moment, the temple curtain is torn in two, symbolizing access to God through Jesus' sacrifice.

Following His death, Jesus is buried in a tomb, but on the third day, He rises from the dead. His resurrection brings hope and victory over sin and death. Jesus appears to His disciples, commissions them to go into all the world and proclaim the Gospel, and then ascends into heaven.

The Gospel of Mark presents Jesus as the suffering servant, the Son of God, who came to redeem humanity through His sacrificial death and resurrection. It calls readers to recognize Jesus' identity, respond in faith, and follow Him wholeheartedly.

Luke

"Luke 19:10 – For the Son of Man came to seek and to save the lost."

The Book of Luke is one of the four Gospels in the New Testament of the Bible. It is traditionally believed to have been written by Luke, a physician and companion of the apostle Paul. Luke's Gospel provides a detailed and comprehensive account of the life, teachings, death, and resurrection of Jesus Christ. Here is a summary of the key themes and events covered in the Book of Luke:

Luke begins by setting the historical context, mentioning the reign of Caesar Augustus and the birth of John the Baptist to an elderly couple, Zechariah and Elizabeth. The angel Gabriel also visits a young virgin named Mary and announces that she will conceive a child by the Holy Spirit, who will be the Savior. Mary and her betrothed husband, Joseph, travel to Bethlehem, where Jesus is born and placed in a manger.

Luke then describes the shepherds who receive the heavenly proclamation of Jesus' birth and visit him. The family later presents Jesus at the temple, where the righteous and devout Simeon and the prophetess Anna recognize him as the fulfillment of God's promises.

As Jesus grows up, Luke briefly mentions his visit to the temple as a young boy, where he impresses the teachers with his understanding. The narrative then jumps to Jesus' adult ministry, beginning with his baptism by John the Baptist in the Jordan River. The Holy Spirit descends upon Jesus, and a voice from heaven declares him to be the beloved Son of God.

Luke emphasizes Jesus' compassion for the marginalized and the outcasts of society. Jesus heals the sick, casts out demons, and performs many miracles, including the feeding of the five thousand and the calming of a storm. He also teaches through parables, illustrating important spiritual truths with relatable stories.

Jesus calls twelve disciples to follow him, and they witness his ministry firsthand. Luke includes notable teachings like the Sermon on the Mount, the Lord's Prayer, and the parables of the Good Samaritan, the Prodigal Son, the Pharisee, and the Tax Collector.

Luke highlights Jesus' interactions with women, emphasizing their dignity and value. He records the stories of the woman who anoints Jesus' feet, the sinful woman who washes his feet with her tears, and the faithful woman who accompanied Jesus during his ministry and witnessed his crucifixion and burial.

As Jesus' popularity grows, so does opposition from religious leaders. They challenge his authority and plot to kill him. Jesus foretells his death and resurrection, and during the Last Supper, he institutes the practice of Communion.

Luke devotes a significant portion of his Gospel to Jesus' betrayal, arrest, trial, crucifixion, and resurrection. He vividly describes Jesus' anguish in the Garden of Gethsemane, his arrest by the religious authorities, and his trial before Pilate. Jesus is crucified alongside criminals, but before he dies, he forgives those who crucify him and promises paradise to a repentant thief.

On the third day after his death, Jesus rises from the dead. He appears to his disciples, explaining the Scriptures and commissioning them to preach the good news to all nations. The Gospel ends with Jesus ascending into heaven, promising the disciples the Holy Spirit, and leaving them with a great mission.

In summary, the Book of Luke presents a detailed account of Jesus' life, ministry, death, and resurrection. It emphasizes Jesus' compassion, his teachings, and his role as the long-awaited Messiah who came to save humanity. Luke's Gospel provides a foundation for understanding the life and significance of Jesus Christ.

John

"John 14:6 – Jesus said to him, "I am the way, and the truth, and the life. No one comes to the Father except through me."

The Book of John is one of the four Gospels in the New Testament of the Bible, providing a unique perspective on the life, ministry, and teachings of Jesus Christ. Written by the apostle John, it emphasizes the divinity of Jesus and his role as the Son of God. The book is divided into several sections, each highlighting different aspects of Jesus' mission and message.

John begins by establishing Jesus' eternal nature as the Word of God, who was with God in the beginning and through whom all things were created. He describes how Jesus, the Word, became flesh and dwelt among humanity, bringing light and life to those who believe in him.

Throughout the book, John narrates a series of miracles or "signs" performed by Jesus to demonstrate his power and divine nature. These signs include turning water into wine, healing the sick, feeding the multitude, walking on water, and raising Lazarus from the dead. Each miracle serves as a revelation of Jesus' authority and an invitation to faith.

In addition to the signs, John also records several "I am" statements made by Jesus, in which he reveals aspects of his identity and purpose. Jesus declares, "I am the bread of life," "I am the light of the world," "I am the door," "I am the good shepherd," "I am the resurrection and the life," "I am the way, the truth, and the life," and "I am the true vine." These statements emphasize his unique role as the source of spiritual nourishment, guidance, and eternal life.

The Book of John also highlights Jesus' interactions with various individuals, such as Nicodemus, a Pharisee who seeks spiritual understanding, and the Samaritan woman at the well, to whom Jesus offers the living water of eternal life. These encounters reveal Jesus' compassion, wisdom, and desire to reach people from all walks of life.

As the narrative progresses, John focuses on Jesus' final days, including his arrest, trial, crucifixion, and resurrection. He portrays Jesus as willingly sacrificing himself as the ultimate atoning sacrifice for the sins of humanity. Through his death and resurrection, Jesus triumphs over sin and death, offering salvation and eternal life to all who believe in him.

The book concludes with an account of Jesus' post-resurrection appearances to his disciples, commissioning them to continue his mission of spreading the Gospel and making disciples of all nations. John ends by emphasizing the purpose of his Gospel, stating that the signs and teachings he recorded were written so that readers may believe in Jesus as the Christ, the Son of God, and have life in his name.

Overall, the Book of John presents a powerful portrait of Jesus as the divine Son of God, who came to bring light, life, and salvation to the world. It invites readers to place their faith in Jesus and experience the transforming power of his love and grace.

Acts

"Acts 1:8 – But you will receive power when the Holy Spirit has come upon you, and you will be my witnesses in Jerusalem and in all Judea and Samaria, and to the end of the earth."

The Book of Acts, also known as the Acts of the Apostles, is a historical narrative in the New Testament of the Bible. It serves as a continuation of the Gospel of Luke and describes the early development of the Christian Church after Jesus' ascension. Here is a summary of the Book of Acts in 500 words or less:

The book begins with Jesus' final instructions to His disciples before His ascension into heaven. He tells them to wait in Jerusalem until they receive the promised Holy Spirit. On the day of Pentecost, the Holy Spirit descended upon the believers, empowering them to speak in different languages and proclaim the message of Jesus to people from various nations. Peter delivers a powerful sermon, leading to the conversion of about 3,000 people.

The early Christian community is characterized by its unity and devotion to teaching, fellowship, prayer, and sharing possessions. Signs and wonders accompany the apostles' ministry, attracting more people to join the growing movement. However, the religious authorities become threatened by the apostles' preaching and perform miracles and imprison them. But an angel miraculously releases them, and they continue to preach fearlessly.

One of the prominent figures in the early Church is Stephen, known for his wisdom and miracles. However, he faces opposition from a group of Jews who accuse him of blasphemy. Stephen delivers a passionate defense of the faith and accuses his accusers of resisting the Holy Spirit throughout Israel's history. Enraged, the crowd stones him to death, making him the first Christian martyr.

Following Stephen's death, a persecution against the Church begins in Jerusalem, led by a young Pharisee named Saul. Saul zealously pursued Christians, arresting them and approving their executions. However, on his way to Damascus, he encounters a blinding light and hears the voice of Jesus, who reveals Himself to Saul and calls him to be His chosen instrument to preach the Gospel to the Gentiles. Saul, later known as the Apostle Paul, underwent a radical transformation and became one of the most influential figures in early Christianity.

The narrative shifts to focus on Paul's missionary journeys. He travels to various cities, preaching in synagogues and public places, and faces both acceptance and opposition. He performs miracles and establishes churches, strengthening the faith of the believers. The apostles and leaders of the early Church convene in Jerusalem to address the issue of Gentile conversion. They conclude that Gentile believers do not need to adhere to Jewish customs and laws but should abstain from certain practices to maintain unity with Jewish believers.

Paul's journeys continue, and he encounters resistance from both Jews and idol-worshipping Gentiles. He faces persecution, imprisonment, and even a shipwreck. Yet, he remains steadfast in his mission to spread the Gospel. Eventually, Paul is arrested in Jerusalem and sent to Rome for trial before Caesar. In Rome, he continues to boldly proclaim the message of Jesus, even while under house arrest.

The book ends with Paul's imprisonment in Rome, but it implies that the Gospel continues to spread and transform lives despite challenges and opposition. Acts portray the early Church's growth, the power of the Holy

Spirit, the faithfulness of the apostles, and the establishment of Christian communities throughout the Roman Empire.

In summary, the Book of Acts recounts the early years of the Christian Church, from the outpouring of the Holy Spirit on Pentecost to the missionary journeys of the Apostle Paul. It highlights the early believers' devotion, the conversion of Saul to Paul, the establishment of Christian communities, and the spread of the Gospel despite persecution and challenges.

Romans

"Romans 1:16 – For I am not ashamed of the gospel, for it is the power of God for salvation to everyone who believes, to the Jew first and also to the Greek."

The Book of Romans is a profound and comprehensive letter written by the apostle Paul to the early Christian community in Rome. In this epistle, Paul addresses a range of theological and practical matters, providing a detailed exposition of the Christian faith and its implications for believers.

Paul begins by asserting the universality of sin, emphasizing that both Jews and Gentiles are equally guilty before God. He explains that righteousness cannot be attained through human effort or adherence to the Law but is instead granted by God through faith in Jesus Christ. Through faith, believers are justified and reconciled with God, receiving the gift of eternal life.

Paul highlights the transformative power of the Gospel, which offers salvation to all who believe, regardless of their background. He emphasizes that salvation is based on faith, not works, and uses the example of Abraham to illustrate this principle. Paul also addresses the role of the Law in God's redemptive plan, explaining that it exposes sin but cannot provide justification. Christ, however, fulfills the Law and grants believers a new life in the Spirit, enabling them to live righteously.

The apostle delves into the significance of Jesus' death and resurrection, emphasizing that through his sacrificial act, believers are set free from the power of sin and death. Paul underscores the transformative work of the

Holy Spirit in the lives of believers, empowering them to live according to God's will and shaping their character to reflect Christ.

In his letter, Paul addresses various practical issues within the Roman Church. He encourages believers to live in harmony, to submit to governing authorities, and to exercise love and hospitality toward one another. He also tackles the challenges of disputes over matters of conscience, urging believers to prioritize unity and not judge one another based on minor disagreements.

Furthermore, Paul emphasizes the role of believers as living sacrifices, urging them to offer their bodies as instruments of righteousness, transformed by the renewing of their minds. He exhorts believers to exhibit genuine love, humility, and service, using their spiritual gifts to build up the body of Christ.

The Book of Romans concludes with Paul expressing his desire to visit Rome and impart spiritual gifts to the believers there. He sends greetings to various individuals and concludes with a majestic doxology, praising God for His wisdom, grace, and the revelation of the mystery of the Gospel.

In summary, the Book of Romans is a rich and profound theological treatise that delves into the universal problem of sin, the grace of God revealed in Jesus Christ, and the transformative power of the Gospel. It emphasizes that salvation is received through faith, not works, and calls believers to live lives of righteousness, love, and service, empowered by the Holy Spirit.

1 Corinthians

"1 Corinthians 10:31 – So, whether you eat or drink, or whatever you do, do all to the glory of God."

The book of 1 Corinthians is a letter written by the apostle Paul to the Church in Corinth, a city in ancient Greece. In this letter, Paul addresses various issues and challenges faced by the Corinthian Church and provides guidance and instructions on matters of faith, morality, and church order.

Paul begins by addressing divisions and conflicts within the Church. He emphasizes the importance of unity among believers, urging them to be united in their faith and not divided by loyalty to different leaders or personal preferences. He emphasizes that the Church is the body of Christ, with each member having a vital role to play.

The letter also deals with the issue of immorality within the Church. Paul condemns sexual immorality and urges believers to flee from it. He addresses specific cases of sexual misconduct and advises the Church on how to discipline those who engage in such behavior.

Paul then tackles the subject of marriage and singleness. He encourages believers to remain faithful in their marital relationships and offers guidance on various issues related to marriage. He also highlights the advantages of remaining single and dedicated to serving the Lord.

The issue of idolatry is another topic addressed in 1 Corinthians. The Corinthian Church was located in a city known for its pagan worship, and some believers were still participating in idolatrous practices. Paul warns against idol worship, emphasizing that believers should only worship the one true God and abstain from any form of idolatry.

The letter also contains instructions regarding the proper conduct of worship services. Paul discusses the use of spiritual gifts, emphasizing that they should be used for the edification and unity of the Church rather than for personal status or self-promotion. He provides guidelines for the orderly exercise of spiritual gifts, especially the gift of speaking in tongues.

Paul addresses various questions raised by the Corinthian believers, including issues related to food sacrificed to idols, head coverings for women in worship, and the proper observance of the Lord's Supper. He provides practical guidance on these matters, seeking to promote unity and godly living within the Church.

Finally, Paul concludes the letter with a powerful chapter on the resurrection of the dead. He affirms the reality of Christ's resurrection and its significance for believers. He assures the Corinthians that just as Christ was raised from the dead, so will believers be raised to eternal life. He encourages them to remain steadfast in their faith and to live in the light of the hope of resurrection.

Overall, the book of 1 Corinthians is a comprehensive and practical letter that addresses the challenges faced by the Corinthian Church. It emphasizes the importance of unity, moral purity, and proper worship. It guides on various issues and encourages believers to live in a manner that glorifies God and reflects the transformative power of the Gospel.

2 Corinthians

"2 Corinthians 5:17 – Therefore, if anyone is in Christ, he is a new creation. The old has passed away; behold, the new has come."

The book of 2 Corinthians, written by the apostle Paul, is a letter addressed to the Christian community in Corinth. It is believed to be the fourth letter Paul wrote to the Corinthians, although some scholars consider it a compilation of multiple letters. The letter, written around 55-56 AD, contains Paul's reflections on his ministry, teachings on Christian ethics, and his defense of his apostleship.

The letter begins with Paul expressing his gratitude to God for comfort and encouragement in his sufferings. He discusses the importance of relying on God's strength in times of weakness and the transformative power of the Gospel. Paul defends his ministry against accusations from some false apostles who criticize his authority and question his integrity.

Paul addresses various issues within the Corinthian Church, including matters of discipline and moral conduct. He urges the Corinthians to forgive and restore a repentant member who had been disciplined previously. He emphasizes the need for sincere repentance and the role of forgiveness in maintaining the unity of the body of Christ.

Paul highlights the surpassing glory of the new covenant in Christ, which surpasses the old covenant of the Law. He contrasts the ministry of the Spirit with the ministry of the letter, emphasizing the importance of the inward transformation of the heart over external appearances. He encourages the Corinthians to live as new creations in Christ, seeking reconciliation and avoiding sinful behavior.

The letter also includes discussions on the topic of giving and generosity. Paul praises the Macedonian churches for their sacrificial giving and encourages the Corinthians to excel in this act of grace. He reminds them that God blesses those who give cheerfully and generously.

Paul defends his apostleship, recounting his sufferings and hardships endured for the sake of the Gospel. He confronts the false apostles who boast about their achievements and credentials, contrasting their self-promotion with his own humble service. Paul emphasizes that true apostleship is marked by selflessness, suffering, and a genuine love for the Church.

In the latter part of the letter, Paul discusses his plans to visit Corinth and expresses his concerns about the spiritual condition of the Church. He warns against false teachers and urges the Corinthians to examine themselves and remain faithful to the truth. He encourages them to embrace the power of Christ, who strengthens believers and enables them to overcome challenges.

In conclusion, 2 Corinthians is a heartfelt letter from Paul to the Corinthian Church. It addresses various issues within the community, including discipline, moral conduct, reconciliation, giving, and the authenticity of his apostleship. Paul emphasizes the power of the Gospel, the importance of a transformed heart, and the need for believers to remain faithful despite challenges. The letter serves as a reminder of God's grace, the centrality of Christ, and the call for believers to live in accordance with the truth of the Gospel.

Galatians

"Galatians 2:20 – I have been crucified with Christ. It is no longer I who live, but Christ who lives in me. And the life I now live in the flesh I live by faith in the Son of God, who loved me and gave himself for me."

The book of Galatians is a letter written by the Apostle Paul to the churches in the region of Galatia. In this powerful and passionate epistle, Paul addresses a critical issue that had arisen among the Galatian Christians—false teachers were spreading a distorted version of the Gospel and urging the believers to embrace a mixture of faith in Christ and observance of the Jewish Law, particularly circumcision.

Paul begins by defending his apostolic authority, stating that he received his Gospel directly from Jesus Christ and not from any human source. He emphasizes that salvation comes through faith in Christ alone, not through adherence to the Law. Paul explains that the Law was given to reveal humanity's sinfulness and our need for a savior. He asserts that we are justified (declared righteous) by faith in Christ and not by works of the Law.

The central theme of Galatians is the contrast between Law and grace, flesh and Spirit. Paul argues that believers have been set free from the bondage of the Law and are now under grace. He uses the example of Abraham to illustrate that even in the Old Testament, justification came through faith and not through the Law. Paul emphasizes that the Law cannot save and that relying on it for righteousness actually brings a curse, as no one can perfectly keep the Law.

Paul urges the Galatians to stand firm in their freedom in Christ and not be burdened again by the yoke of slavery to the Law. He warns them about the danger of allowing false teachers to lead them astray and reminds them that true faith works through love. He encourages them to live by the Spirit and to produce the fruit of the Spirit, which includes love, joy, peace, patience, kindness, goodness, faithfulness, gentleness, and self-control.

Paul emphasizes the importance of unity among believers and calls them to bear one another's burdens and restore those who have fallen. He instructs them to fulfill the Law of Christ by loving one another and treating each other with kindness and gentleness.

In the closing part of the letter, Paul highlights the cross of Christ as the only ground for boasting. He declares that he bears in his body the marks of Jesus, meaning that he has suffered for the sake of the Gospel. He emphasizes that what matters is a new creation—being transformed by the Spirit, not outward circumcision or adherence to the Law.

The book of Galatians is a passionate defense of the Gospel of grace and a strong warning against legalism. It emphasizes that salvation is a gift of God's grace received through faith in Christ, and it calls believers to live in freedom and love, guided by the Holy Spirit. It is a powerful reminder that our righteousness and acceptance before God come not from our own efforts but through the finished work of Christ on the cross.

Ephesians

"Ephesians 2:8 – For by grace you have been saved through faith. And this is not your own doing; it is the gift of God,"

The Book of Ephesians is an epistle written by the apostle Paul to the Church in Ephesus, a city in ancient Asia Minor (modern-day Turkey). It consists of six chapters and covers a variety of themes, including the identity of believers in Christ, the unity of the Church, and the practical implications of Christian living. Here is a summary of the key messages found in the book:

In the opening chapter, Paul emphasizes the blessings and spiritual riches that believers have in Christ. He highlights the predestination of believers, their adoption as God's children, and the sealing of the Holy Spirit as a guarantee of their future inheritance. Paul's prayer for the Ephesian believers is that they may have wisdom, knowledge, and a deeper understanding of God's purposes.

Moving into the second chapter, Paul discusses the nature of salvation by grace through faith. He emphasizes that salvation is not based on one's works but is a gift from God. Moreover, he emphasizes the unity between Jews and Gentiles in the body of Christ, breaking down the barriers that had historically separated them.

In the following chapters, Paul addresses the practical implications of this unity. He urges believers to live a life worthy of their calling, walking in love, humility, and unity. He encourages them to put off their old way of life, characterized by darkness and sin, and to embrace the new life in Christ, characterized by righteousness and holiness.

Paul also highlights the importance of unity and diversity within the body of Christ. He uses the metaphor of the Church as a body, with Christ as the head and individual believers as its members. Each member has unique gifts and contributions to make, and together, they form a harmonious and functioning body.

In the later chapters, Paul addresses the relationships within the Christian household. He provides instructions for husbands and wives, parents and children, and slaves and masters, emphasizing mutual love, respect, and submission. He encourages believers to be filled with the Spirit and to engage in spiritual warfare against the forces of evil.

Overall, the Book of Ephesians emphasizes the grandeur of God's plan of salvation, the unity and diversity within the body of Christ, and the practical implications of living as believers in a fallen world. It calls believers to embrace their identity in Christ, to walk in love and unity, and to live out their faith in all aspects of life. The book serves as a guide for believers to understand the rich blessings they have received and to live in a manner worthy of the Gospel.

Philippians

Philippians 3:7 – But whatever gain I had, I counted as loss for the sake of Christ.

The Book of Philippians, written by the Apostle Paul, is a letter addressed to the Christian community in the city of Philippi. Despite being imprisoned at the time, Paul's letter is filled with joy, encouragement, and exhortation to the believers. In this book, he expresses his gratitude for their partnership in the Gospel and provides instructions on Christian living and unity within the church.

Paul begins by expressing his deep affection for the Philippians and their shared commitment to the Gospel. He encourages them to continue growing in their faith and to stand firm in the face of persecution and challenges. He emphasizes the importance of humility, selflessness, and considering others above oneself, pointing to the example of Jesus Christ, who humbled Himself and became obedient unto death.

The Apostle urges the Philippians to work out their salvation with fear and trembling, reminding them that it is God who works in them to will and to act according to His good purpose. He encourages them to shine as lights in the world, holding fast to the word of life and rejoicing in their faith, even in the midst of difficult circumstances.

Paul addresses the issue of division within the church and encourages the Philippians to be of one mind and to put the interests of others before their own. He mentions two individuals, Euodia and Syntyche, and urges them to reconcile their differences and work together for the sake of the Gospel. Paul emphasizes the need for unity, love, and harmonious relationships among believers.

The Apostle warns the Philippians against false teachings and encourages them to remain steadfast in their faith. He emphasizes the surpassing value of knowing Christ and shares his personal desire to know Him more intimately. Paul acknowledges his own imperfections and presses on toward the goal of attaining the resurrection from the dead.

In the latter part of the letter, Paul expresses his gratitude for the financial support the Philippians have provided him during his imprisonment. He assures them that their generosity is not in vain and promises that God will supply all their needs according to His riches in Christ Jesus.

The letter concludes with greetings and blessings to various individuals in the Philippian church. Paul sends his love and greetings to the saints and encourages them to rejoice in the Lord always. He urges them to think about whatever is true, noble, correct, pure, lovely, admirable, excellent, or praiseworthy and to put into practice the things they have learned from him.

Overall, the Book of Philippians is a letter filled with encouragement, exhortation, and practical advice for Christian living. It emphasizes the joy that comes from knowing Christ and the importance of unity, humility, and love within the body of believers. Paul's words continue to inspire and guide Christians today, encouraging them to live out their faith with joy and purpose.

Colossians

Colossians 3:2 – Set your minds on things that are above, not on things that are on earth.

The Book of Colossians, written by the Apostle Paul, is a letter addressed to the Christian community in the city of Colossae. In this letter, Paul emphasizes the preeminence of Christ and addresses various issues faced by the Colossian believers.

Paul begins by expressing his gratitude to God for the faith and love that the Colossian Christians have shown. He then proceeds to exalt Christ as the image of the invisible God and the creator and sustainer of all things. Paul emphasizes that Christ holds supremacy in all things, including the spiritual realm, and that all believers should submit to His authority.

The letter also addresses the issue of false teachings that had infiltrated the Colossian church. Paul warns against the deceptive philosophy and empty deceit promoted by false teachers. He urges the believers to hold fast to the truth of the Gospel and not be led astray by human tradition or elemental spirits.

Paul highlights the fullness and sufficiency of Christ, stating that in Him, the fullness of God dwells bodily. He encourages the Colossian believers to live in Christ, rooted and built up in Him, and to reject any teachings that diminish His preeminence.

Paul then proceeds to provide practical instructions on how believers should live in light of their union with Christ. He encourages them to put off their old selves and put on the new self, characterized by compassion, kindness, humility, meekness, and patience. He emphasizes the importance of forgiveness, love, and thankfulness in their relationships with one another.

The letter also addresses specific issues within the Colossian church. Paul instructs masters and slaves on how to relate to one another in a Christ-honoring manner. He urges them to treat one another justly and fairly, recognizing that their ultimate Master is in heaven.

Paul concludes the letter with personal greetings and instructions for the Colossian believers. He requests their prayers for his ministry and encourages them to make the most of every opportunity to share the Gospel. He also sends greetings from fellow workers and instructs the Colossians to share his letter with the neighboring church in Laodicea.

In summary, the Book of Colossians highlights the preeminence of Christ, warns against false teachings, and provides practical instructions for Christian living. It emphasizes the fullness and sufficiency of Christ and urges believers to live in Him, rooted and built up in faith. Paul's letter encourages unity, love, and thankfulness among believers and guides various aspects of Christian life, including relationships, work, and evangelism.

1 Thessalonians

1 Thessalonians 5:2 – For you yourselves are fully aware that the day of the Lord will come like a thief in the night.

The book of 1 Thessalonians is a letter written by the Apostle Paul to the early Christian community in Thessalonica. Paul wrote this letter to encourage and strengthen the believers in their faith, address some concerns, and provide instructions for holy living and the second coming of Christ.

In the opening of the letter, Paul expresses his gratitude for the Thessalonians' faith and their perseverance in the face of persecution. He reminds them of their conversion to Christianity and commends them for their positive example to other believers in the region.

Paul then addresses the concern of the Thessalonians about the fate of those who have died before the second coming of Christ. He assures them that those who have died in Christ will rise again when Jesus returns, and they will be reunited with Him. This message brings comfort to the Thessalonians, who were grieving the loss of their fellow believers.

The Apostle also addresses the importance of living a holy life, urging the Thessalonians to abstain from sexual immorality and to love one another. He encourages them to lead a quiet life, work diligently, and be responsible members of society. Paul emphasizes the importance of maintaining a strong and honorable reputation among outsiders.

Furthermore, Paul addresses the issue of idleness and laziness among some believers. He instructs them to work with their own hands and be self-sufficient so as not to be a burden to others. He reminds them of his own example of hard work while he was with them.

In the later part of the letter, Paul turns his attention to the second coming of Christ, a topic that had confused the Thessalonians. He assures them that Jesus will return in glory, and the resurrection of the dead will accompany this event. Paul describes the events that will occur during Christ's return and emphasizes the need for readiness and watchfulness. He encourages them to live in hope and to comfort one another with these words.

In conclusion, the book of 1 Thessalonians is a letter of encouragement, exhortation, and instruction from Paul to the early Christian community in Thessalonica. Paul commends their faith, addresses their concerns about death and the second coming of Christ, and provides guidance on holy living and responsible conduct. The overarching theme is to remain faithful, live in love and holiness, and eagerly await the return of Jesus Christ.

2 Thessalonians

2 Thessalonians 3:3 – But the Lord is faithful. He will establish you and guard you against the evil one.

The Book of 2 Thessalonians is one of the letters written by the Apostle Paul to the early Christian community in Thessalonica. It serves as a sequel to his first letter to the Thessalonians and addresses some of the concerns and questions that arose after his initial correspondence.

The letter begins by expressing gratitude for the Thessalonians' faithfulness and endurance in the midst of persecution. Paul commends them for their growth in faith and encourages them to continue living according to the teachings they had received from him. He reassures them that God will judge those who afflict them and grant them relief when Jesus returns.

Paul then turns his attention to addressing a misunderstanding among the Thessalonians concerning the return of Christ. Some believers were under the impression that the day of the Lord had already come, leading to confusion and fear. Paul clarifies that certain events must occur before Christ's return, including the rise of a "man of lawlessness" or the "son of perdition" who exalts himself above God. He warns the Thessalonians to be vigilant and not be deceived by false teachings or signs, emphasizing the necessity of holding onto the truth of the Gospel.

Furthermore, Paul reminds the Thessalonians of his previous teachings and encourages them to work diligently, earn their own living, and avoid idleness. He sets an example by laboring while he is with them so as not to be a burden on anyone. Paul stresses the importance of community, urging them to live in harmony, love one another, and correct those who are idle or disruptive.

The Apostle then offers a prayer for the Thessalonians, asking God to comfort and strengthen them in their faith and for the Lord to guide their hearts into His love and perseverance. He concludes by urging them to stand firm in their beliefs and to stay away from anyone who disregards his teachings.

In summary, the Book of 2 Thessalonians addresses the concerns of the Thessalonian believers and provides guidance and encouragement in their faith. It clarifies misconceptions about the return of Christ, warns against deception, and emphasizes the need for steadfastness and unity within the community. Paul's words serve as a reminder of the importance of staying true to the teachings of Christ and remaining hopeful in the face of adversity.

1 Timothy

1 Timothy 4:16 – Keep a close watch on yourself and on the teaching. Persist in this, for by so doing, you will save both yourself and your hearers.

The Book of 1 Timothy is a letter written by the apostle Paul to his disciple Timothy, providing guidance and instructions for his ministry in Ephesus. The letter addresses various issues concerning church leadership, false teachings, and personal conduct within the Christian community.

Paul begins by reminding Timothy of his purpose in Ephesus, encouraging him to remain faithful in his calling despite any challenges he may face. He emphasizes the importance of sound doctrine and warns against false teachers who promote speculations and controversies rather than the pure gospel message.

Paul then addresses the roles and qualifications of leaders within the church. He outlines the qualifications for overseers (also known as elders or bishops) and deacons, stressing the importance of their character, integrity, and ability to manage their own households well. These leaders should be examples to the rest of the congregation and have a deep understanding of the gospel.

In regards to the role of women in the church, Paul instructs them to learn quietly and with submission, stating that he does not permit women to have authority over men in teaching or exercising authority. This has been a point of debate among scholars, with various interpretations proposed.

Paul also addresses the issue of public worship, encouraging men to pray with uplifted hands and women to dress modestly and adorn themselves with good works rather than extravagant attire. He emphasizes the importance of modesty, good deeds, and a proper understanding of God's design for men and women.

The apostle then warns Timothy about the dangers of material wealth and the love of money. He states that the love of money is the root of all kinds of evil and encourages contentment and generosity. Paul advises Timothy to be content with the basic necessities of life and to pursue righteousness, godliness, faith, love, endurance, and gentleness.

In the latter part of the letter, Paul addresses various instructions for the church community. He emphasizes the importance of praying for all people, including political leaders, and highlights the role of Jesus Christ as the mediator between God and humanity. Paul also addresses the responsibilities of widows, instructing the church to care for those who are truly in need.

Lastly, Paul advises Timothy regarding the use of alcohol and the treatment of elders in the church. He encourages Timothy to practice discernment and not to hastily ordain new leaders, as this could lead to their potential downfall.

In summary, the Book of 1 Timothy offers practical guidance for church leadership, the conduct of believers, and the importance of sound doctrine. It addresses issues such as false teaching, qualifications for leaders, the role of women, the dangers of material wealth, and proper behavior within the church community. Paul's teachings aim to establish order, maintain the integrity of the gospel, and encourage godly living among believers.

2 Timothy

2 Timothy 3:16 – All Scripture is breathed out by God and profitable for teaching, for reproof, for correction, and for training in righteousness.

The Book of 2 Timothy is a letter written by the apostle Paul to his beloved disciple Timothy. It serves as Paul's final words of encouragement and exhortation to Timothy, providing guidance and instructions for his ministry. The letter emphasizes the importance of perseverance, faithfulness, and sound doctrine in the face of challenges and opposition.

Paul begins by expressing his gratitude for Timothy's sincere faith and the legacy of faith passed down to him from his grandmother, Lois, and his mother, Eunice. He encourages Timothy to fan into flame the gift of God that was bestowed upon him and to not be discouraged by any hardships that may come his way. Paul reminds Timothy that God has not given him a spirit of fear but of power, love, and self-discipline.

The apostle emphasizes the importance of sound teaching and doctrine, warning Timothy about false teachers and their deceptive ways. Paul urges him to hold fast to the truth and to guard the gospel entrusted to him. He encourages Timothy to study and rightly handle the Word of God, being diligent in his efforts to present himself as an approved workman before God.

Paul highlights his own imminent death and expresses his readiness to be poured out as a drink offering. He urges Timothy to join him in enduring suffering for the sake of the gospel, reminding him that those who endure will also reign with Christ. The apostle provides examples of individuals who have turned away from him, but he also mentions those who have remained faithful, such as Onesiphorus, who ministered to Paul in his time of need.

In his letter, Paul urges Timothy to be strong and courageous, reminding him of his calling and the grace of God that empowers him. He encourages him to avoid quarrels and foolish arguments, instead pursuing righteousness, faith, love, and peace. Paul advises Timothy to avoid sinful desires and to pursue godliness, reminding him of the importance of fleeing from youthful passions and pursuing righteousness, faith, love, and peace.

The apostle concludes his letter by requesting Timothy's presence and urging him to come quickly. He sends greetings to various individuals, both encouraging and warning about specific people who have caused him harm. Paul emphasizes the importance of the Lord's presence and strength in all things and prays for God's mercy to be upon Timothy.

In summary, the Book of 2 Timothy serves as a heartfelt letter from Paul to Timothy, providing guidance and encouragement for his ministry. It emphasizes the importance of perseverance, sound doctrine, and faithfulness in the face of opposition. Paul urges Timothy to remain strong, avoid false teachings, and diligently pursue righteousness, love, and peace. The letter concludes with personal requests, greetings, and prayers for God's mercy.

Titus

Titus 3:5 – he saved us, not because of works done by us in righteousness, but according to his own mercy, by the washing of regeneration and renewal of the Holy Spirit.

The Book of Titus is a short letter found in the New Testament of the Bible, attributed to the apostle Paul. It is addressed to Titus, a fellow worker and trusted companion of Paul, and provides instructions on leadership and conduct within the Christian community. Here is a summary of the key themes and teachings presented in the Book:

The letter begins with Paul highlighting his apostolic authority and acknowledging Titus as his true child in a common faith. Paul then reveals the purpose of the letter, which is to instruct Titus in his role as an overseer in the church, specifically on the island of Crete.

Paul emphasizes the importance of sound doctrine and urges Titus to appoint qualified elders who are above reproach, faithful in their marriages, and capable of teaching and guiding others. These leaders should be people of good character, free from the love of money and excessive indulgence.

Paul addresses various groups within the church, offering specific instructions on how they should conduct themselves. He encourages older men to be sober-minded, self-controlled, and sound in faith, love, and patience. Likewise, he instructs older women to be reverent in behavior, not slanderers or addicted to wine, but rather teachers of good things and examples to the younger women.

Paul directs Titus to teach the younger men to exercise self-control, showing integrity and sound speech that cannot be condemned. He also highlights the importance of slaves or employees showing respect and obedience to their masters or employers, promoting a positive witness for the Christian faith.

Throughout the letter, Paul emphasizes the transformative power of God's grace, which leads to salvation and instructs believers to deny ungodliness and live upright, godly lives in the present age. He emphasizes the significance of Jesus Christ's redemptive work and the hope of eternal life that believers have through Him.

Additionally, Paul encourages Titus to stress the importance of good works and to remind the congregation to be ready for every good work, to be subject to authorities, and to speak evil of no one.

The letter concludes with Paul's instructions for Titus to meet him in Nicopolis, where he intends to spend the winter. Paul sends greetings and conveys his final exhortations, urging the believers to learn to devote themselves to good works, as this is profitable and beneficial for all.

In summary, the Book of Titus focuses on the qualities and behaviors expected of leaders within the church, as well as the general conduct and character of believers. It emphasizes the significance of sound doctrine, good works, and living in a manner that reflects the transformative power of God's grace.

Philemon

Philemon 1:6 – and I pray that the sharing of your faith may become effective for the full knowledge of every good thing that is in us for the sake of Christ.

The Book of Philemon is a brief letter written by the apostle Paul to Philemon, a Christian slave owner. It is one of Paul's prison epistles and is believed to have been written during his imprisonment in Rome around 60-62 AD. The letter primarily addresses the issue of Onesimus, a runaway slave who had become a Christian under Paul's ministry.

The letter begins with Paul expressing his gratitude and prayers for Philemon, acknowledging his love for the saints and his faith in Jesus Christ. Paul then introduces the main purpose of his letter: to appeal to Philemon on behalf of Onesimus, who has now become a valuable fellow worker for Paul during his imprisonment. Paul refers to Onesimus as his "child," indicating the spiritual transformation that has taken place in the slave's life.

Paul reveals that Onesimus had previously been unprofitable to Philemon, presumably by running away. However, now that he has become a Christian, Paul appeals to Philemon to receive him back, not as a slave but as a beloved brother in Christ. Paul demonstrates his deep concern for the reconciliation and restoration of their relationship by saying that if Onesimus owes anything or has caused any harm, Philemon should charge it to Paul's account.

The letter showcases Paul's persuasive and diplomatic skills as he tries to convince Philemon to receive Onesimus with love and forgiveness. He emphasizes the value of their newfound brotherhood in Christ, appealing to Philemon's faith and Christian duty to forgive and reconcile. Paul mentions that he is confident in Philemon's obedience and hints at his desire to visit him in the future, implying that he expects Philemon to respond favorably to his appeal.

In addition to addressing Philemon directly, Paul also includes the recipients of the letter—Apphia, Archippus, and the church that meets in Philemon's house. He encourages them to support Philemon's decision and receive Onesimus with open arms, further strengthening the appeal for unity and reconciliation.

The Book of Philemon serves as a powerful example of Paul's approach to resolving conflicts within the early Christian community. It highlights the transformative power of the gospel and its implications for relationships, particularly in the context of slavery. Paul's letter seeks to dismantle the barriers and prejudices that existed between slaves and their masters, promoting equality and unity among believers.

While the Book of Philemon is short and focused on a specific situation, its underlying message of forgiveness, reconciliation, and the power of Christian love resonates beyond its immediate context. It reminds believers of the importance of extending grace and compassion to one another, regardless of social status or past wrongs, and encourages them to pursue unity and reconciliation in Christ.

Hebrews

Hebrews 12:2 – looking to Jesus, the founder, and perfecter of our faith, who for the joy that was set before him endured the cross, despising the shame, and is seated at the right hand of the throne of God.

The Book of Hebrews is a profound letter in the New Testament of the Bible. Though its author remains uncertain, its message and teachings are of great significance. Hebrews addresses a primarily Jewish audience, urging them to remain faithful to Jesus Christ and not revert back to Judaism. It emphasizes the superiority of Christ and the new covenant He has established.

The Book begins by highlighting Jesus' superiority over angels, as He is the Son of God. It emphasizes that Jesus is the radiance of God's glory and the exact representation of His nature. Throughout the letter, the author compares Jesus to various figures and institutions from the Old Testament, demonstrating His superiority in every aspect.

The Book then proceeds to compare Jesus to Moses, the great leader of Israel. While Moses was faithful as a servant in God's house, Jesus is the Son and the builder of a greater house. Jesus' role as the High Priest is also emphasized, as He surpasses the Levitical priesthood by offering Himself as the ultimate sacrifice for the forgiveness of sins. His sacrifice is superior to the animal sacrifices of the Old Covenant, bringing about a new and better covenant.

Hebrews highlights the faith of the Old Testament heroes and encourages the readers to persevere in their own faith journey. It warns against the danger of falling away from the truth and encourages believers to hold fast to their confidence in Christ. The Book offers various exhortations, such as the importance of entering God's rest and the need for mutual love and support within the Christian community.

The author emphasizes the significance of faith throughout Hebrews. Faith is described as the assurance of things hoped for and the conviction of things not seen. The heroes of the Old Testament demonstrated great faith, and the readers were encouraged to follow their example. The letter also emphasizes the importance of endurance and perseverance in the face of trials and tribulations.

The Book of Hebrews concludes with a call to worship God with reverence and awe. The readers are reminded that God is a consuming fire and that they should offer Him acceptable worship. The author expresses his desire for the readers to be equipped with everything good to do God's will, and he prays for their restoration.

In summary, the Book of Hebrews is a powerful letter that urges its readers to remain faithful to Jesus Christ. It highlights His superiority over angels, Moses, and the Levitical priesthood. It emphasizes the significance of faith, endurance, and perseverance in the Christian life. Ultimately, Hebrews encourages believers to worship God with reverence and live in accordance with His will.

James

James 2:17 – So also faith by itself, if it does not have works, is dead.

The Book of James, found in the New Testament of the Bible, is attributed to James, the brother of Jesus. It is a practical and highly ethical letter written to Jewish-Christian communities scattered throughout the Roman Empire. James emphasizes the importance of genuine faith and its expression through good works.

James begins by urging believers to consider trials as opportunities for growth and to ask God for wisdom. He encourages them to persevere through hardships as these trials refine their faith and produce endurance. James emphasizes the need for consistency in seeking wisdom from God rather than being double-minded or relying on earthly riches.

The letter then addresses the issue of favoritism and discrimination within the Christian community. James warns against showing partiality based on wealth or social status, emphasizing the equality of all believers before God. He highlights the inconsistency of showing preferential treatment to the wealthy while neglecting the poor. True faith, according to James, is demonstrated by treating others with love and kindness.

James also addresses the power of words and the importance of controlling one's tongue. He warns against the destructive nature of gossip, slander, and cursing. Instead, he encourages believers to speak words of encouragement, truth, and blessing. He emphasizes that faith without self-control over one's speech is useless.

The letter then turns to the relationship between faith and works. James counters the notion that faith alone is sufficient for salvation, arguing that true faith is accompanied by good works. He provides examples of faith in action, highlighting Abraham and Rahab as individuals whose faith led them to demonstrate their beliefs through their actions.

James also emphasizes the importance of practical love and care for others, particularly the vulnerable and marginalized. He condemns the mistreatment of the poor, widows, and orphans, calling believers to actively demonstrate their faith by providing for their needs. He stresses that faith must be active, showing itself in deeds of compassion and mercy.

The Book concludes with exhortations on the power of prayer, the restoration of those who have wandered from the truth, and the importance of confessing sins to one another. James encourages believers to be patient and to live in anticipation of the Lord's return. He emphasizes the value of righteous living, correcting those who have strayed from the path of truth, and seeking reconciliation within the community.

In summary, the Book of James emphasizes the integration of faith and works. It calls believers to live out their faith through practical acts of love, demonstrating genuine faith through deeds of mercy, kindness, and justice. James encourages believers to be humble, slow to anger, quick to listen, and careful with their words. Ultimately, the Book of James challenges readers to embrace a faith that transforms their lives and impacts the world around them.

1 Peter

1 Peter 5:7 – casting all your anxieties on him, because he cares for you.

The Book of 1 Peter is a letter written by the apostle Peter addressed to the Christian believers scattered throughout various regions. It offers encouragement and guidance in the face of suffering and persecution. Here is a summary of the Book in 500 words or less:

Peter begins his letter by addressing the recipients as exiles, emphasizing their identity as chosen people of God, redeemed by the blood of Jesus Christ. He praises God for their living hope and the inheritance that awaits them in heaven, reminding them of the imperishable nature of their faith.

Peter encourages the believers to endure their trials with patience, highlighting the refining process that suffering brings. He urges them to live holy lives, loving one another deeply and conducting themselves in a manner that brings glory to God. He advises them to abstain from worldly passions and desires, instead pursuing righteousness and living as obedient children of God.

The apostle emphasizes the believers' position as a chosen and royal priesthood called to proclaim the excellencies of God. He encourages them to submit to the governing authorities, to honor everyone, and to show respect to all, including slaves to their masters. Peter emphasizes the importance of displaying Christ-like character and behavior, even in the face of mistreatment.

Peter addresses the theme of suffering in more detail, stating that believers should not be surprised by the fiery trials they face. He reminds them that they share in the sufferings of Christ, and their faith will be tested like gold. He encourages them to rejoice in their suffering, knowing that it refines their faith and ultimately brings glory to God.

The apostle then provides practical instructions for the believers in their relationships. He addresses the roles of husbands and wives, urging husbands to honor their wives and wives to submit to their husbands. Peter emphasizes the importance of humility and unity among believers, urging them to serve one another, show love, and be compassionate.

Peter warns the believers about the devil, who seeks to devour and destroy them. He urges them to be alert and self-controlled, resisting the devil and standing firm in their faith. He reminds them that their fellow believers around the world are also undergoing similar suffering, encouraging them to find strength and solidarity in their shared experiences.

In the closing section of the letter, Peter encourages the elders to shepherd the flock of God with humility and diligence. He advises the younger members to submit to the elders and to clothe themselves with humility in their interactions with one another. Peter concludes by exhorting the believers to cast their anxieties on God, knowing that He cares for them and reminding them of the grace and peace found in Christ.

In summary, the Book of 1 Peter offers guidance and encouragement to Christian believers facing persecution and suffering. It emphasizes the importance of enduring trials with patience, living holy lives, and demonstrating Christ-like character. It reminds believers of their identity in Christ and encourages them to find strength in their shared experiences and their hope of eternal inheritance.

2 Peter

"2 Peter 3:18 – But grow in the grace and knowledge of our Lord and Savior Jesus Christ. To him be the glory both now and to the day of eternity. Amen."

The book of 2 Peter is a short letter written by the apostle Peter, likely in the final years of his life. It is addressed to a group of Christians facing false teachings and moral challenges. The letter emphasizes the importance of knowing and living according to the true knowledge of Jesus Christ.

Peter begins by urging his readers to grow in their faith and to embrace godly virtues. He encourages them to make every effort to add to their faith, goodness, knowledge, self-control, perseverance, godliness, brotherly kindness, and love. He emphasizes that these qualities will keep them from being ineffective and unproductive in their understanding of Jesus.

Peter warns the believers about false teachers who will come and try to distort the truth. He describes these false teachers as having destructive doctrines and immoral lifestyles. He reminds the readers of God's judgment on the wicked in the past and assures them that these false teachers will also face judgment.

The apostle emphasizes the reliability of the Scriptures, stating that they were not produced by human will but rather by men inspired by the Holy Spirit. He encourages the believers to pay close attention to the prophetic word, as it serves as a light in a dark world.

Peter reminds his readers of the Day of the Lord, a future event when Jesus will return to judge the world. He describes the judgment as a purifying fire that will destroy the heavens and the earth, making way for a new heaven and a new earth where righteousness will dwell.

The apostle addresses scoffers who doubt the Second Coming of Jesus. He assures the believers that God is patient, desiring that all should come to repentance. He encourages them to live in holiness and godliness, eagerly awaiting the day of God's judgment.

Peter warns against the influence of false teachers who promote licentiousness and deny the coming judgment, describing them as slaves of corruption. He compares their fate to that of Sodom and Gomorrah. He emphasizes the importance of staying steadfast in the truth and growing in the grace and knowledge of Jesus Christ.

In conclusion, Peter exhorts his readers to be on guard against deception and to continue growing in their faith. He encourages them to be diligent, aware of the dangers of false teachings, and to hold firm to the truth of the Gospel. The letter of 2 Peter serves as a reminder of the importance of living a godly life, being prepared for Christ's return, and relying on the Scriptures as a trustworthy guide in the midst of challenges and opposition.

1 John

"1 John 1:9 – If we confess our sins, he is faithful and just to forgive us our sins and to cleanse us from all unrighteousness."

The book of 1 John is a letter written by the apostle John to a community of believers. It carries important themes of love, fellowship, and obedience to God's commandments. In this summary, I will highlight the key points and messages conveyed in this book.

The central theme of 1 John is the assurance of eternal life in Christ and the importance of genuine fellowship with God and fellow believers. John begins by emphasizing his firsthand experience with Jesus, emphasizing the reality of Jesus' incarnation and the significance of His sacrifice for the forgiveness of sins.

John stresses the importance of living in the light and walking in righteousness as a response to God's love. He emphasizes that love is the defining characteristic of those who abide in God. He encourages believers to love one another, showing that love is not just a sentiment but an active choice to act in love towards others.

John addresses the issue of false teachers who were trying to deceive the community. He warns the believers to discern the spirits and test the teachings they encounter, reminding them that the Spirit of God resides within them and guides them into truth. He encourages them to hold on to the truth they have received and to reject any form of deception.

Furthermore, John highlights the importance of obedience to God's commandments. He stresses that genuine love for God is demonstrated through obedience and that those who claim to know God but do not keep

His commandments are not truly in a relationship with Him. John also reminds believers of the power of confession and forgiveness, encouraging them to confess their sins to God and receive His cleansing and forgiveness.

Throughout the letter, John addresses the issue of assurance of salvation. He assures the believers that those who have faith in Jesus Christ have eternal life and can have confidence in their relationship with God. He emphasizes the role of the Holy Spirit in confirming their faith and testifying to their adoption as children of God.

John concludes by highlighting the victory believers have over the world through their faith in Jesus Christ. He encourages them to trust in God, persist in prayer, and support one another in their journey of faith.

In summary, the book of 1 John focuses on the themes of love, fellowship, obedience, and assurance of salvation. John calls believers to love one another, discern false teachings, walk in obedience to God's commandments, and find assurance of their salvation through faith in Jesus Christ. The letter serves as a guide for believers to deepen their relationship with God, experience true fellowship with one another, and live in the light as children of God.

2

3 John

"2 John 1:6 – And this is love, that we walk according to his commandments; this is the commandment, just as you have heard from the beginning, so that you should walk in it."

The book of 2 John is one of the shorter letters in the New Testament, consisting of only 13 verses. It is addressed to *"the chosen lady and her children,"* though the exact identity of the recipients remains uncertain. The letter is attributed to the apostle John and focuses on the themes of truth, love, and the danger of false teachings.

The author begins by expressing his joy in discovering that some of the recipients' children are walking in the truth, living according to the commandments they received from the Father. He emphasizes the importance of love in following these commandments, stating that love is not a new commandment but one that they have had from the beginning.

The main concern of the letter is the warning against false teachers. The author urges the readers to be vigilant and discerning to ensure that they do not receive or support anyone who does not confess the true teachings of Jesus Christ. He emphasizes that those who deny Jesus' divinity and humanity or who distort his teachings are deceivers and antichrists.

Furthermore, the author advises the chosen lady and her children not to offer hospitality or support to these false teachers. By doing so, they would become participants in their evil deeds. Instead, they are encouraged to continue in their love for one another, abiding by the teaching of Christ.

The letter concludes by expressing the author's desire to visit them in person and to have a face-to-face conversation. He closes with greetings from the chosen lady's sister and sends greetings from *"the children of your sister, chosen by God."*

In summary, 2 John is a short but powerful letter that emphasizes the importance of truth, love, and discernment in the face of false teachings. The author encourages the recipients to remain faithful to the teachings of Jesus Christ and warns against supporting those who deviate from the truth. The letter serves as a reminder to stay firm in their faith and to continue living in love and obedience to God's commandments.

4 John

"3 John 1:4 – I have no greater joy than to hear that my children are walking in the truth."

The book of 3 John is a short letter in the New Testament of the Bible written by the apostle John. It is addressed to a man named Gaius and serves as a personal and pastoral encouragement to him. The letter touches upon themes of hospitality, truth, and the importance of supporting fellow believers.

The letter begins with John expressing his joy upon hearing that Gaius is walking in the truth and living according to the commandments of God. He commends Gaius for his hospitality and his support of itinerant missionaries who have come to preach the Gospel. John emphasizes the importance of showing love and support to these messengers of Christ as they journey in the service of the Lord.

John then contrasts the hospitality shown by Gaius with the actions of a man named Diotrephes, who is described as power-hungry and unwilling to receive the traveling missionaries. Diotrephes even goes so far as to spread malicious gossip about John and other leaders within the early Christian community. John warns Gaius not to imitate Diotrephes' negative behavior but rather to follow the example of those who do good.

The apostle encourages Gaius to persevere in his faith and to continue doing what is right. He reassures him that he will personally address the situation with Diotrephes when he visits. John hopes to restore order and ensure that truth and love prevail within the community.

Furthermore, John praises a man named Demetrius, commending his good reputation among the believers. It is possible that Demetrius was a trusted envoy who carried this letter to Gaius and served as a witness to the truth of John's words.

In conclusion, the book of 3 John conveys a message of encouragement, emphasizing the importance of hospitality, truth, and support for fellow believers. It warns against the negative influence of individuals like Diotrephes, who seek power and sow division within the community. The letter encourages Gaius to continue his faithful walk and assures him of John's involvement in addressing the issues at hand. Overall, 3 John reminds believers of the importance of living in truth, extending hospitality, and supporting those who faithfully serve the Gospel.

Jude

"Jude 1:21 – keep yourselves in the love of God, waiting for the mercy of our Lord Jesus Christ that leads to eternal life."

The book of Jude is a short letter found in the New Testament of the Bible. It is attributed to Jude, the brother of James and a servant of Jesus Christ. It's written to a specific audience, as Jude's letter addresses the urgent need to contend for the faith and warns against false teachers who have infiltrated the church.

Jude begins by expressing his initial intention to write about salvation but feels compelled to address the pressing issue of false teachers corrupting the faith. He urges his readers to ***"contend earnestly for the faith which was once for all delivered to the saints" (Jude 1:3).*** The faith Jude refers to encompasses the core teachings of Christianity and the gospel message.

He illustrates his concern by reminding the readers of the historical examples of God's judgment upon those who rejected His authority. Jude warns that just as God punished rebellious angels, the wicked in Sodom and Gomorrah, and the Israelites who rebelled in the wilderness, these false teachers will face severe judgment for their ungodly behavior.

Jude proceeds to describe the characteristics and actions of these false teachers. They distort God's grace, deny the lordship of Jesus Christ, and indulge in sexual immorality. Their desires drive them, and they exhibit arrogance and blasphemy. Despite their outward religious appearance, Jude declares that they are devoid of the Spirit of God.

To emphasize the gravity of their actions, Jude references various historical and biblical examples. He mentions the archangel Michael disputing with the devil over the body of Moses and the prophecy of Enoch regarding the judgment of the ungodly. These references emphasize the certainty and severity of God's judgment upon those who pervert the truth.

Jude encourages his readers to remain steadfast in their faith and build themselves up in the holiest faith, praying in the Holy Spirit. He urges them to show mercy to those who doubt and to reach out to those who have been influenced by the false teachers, seeking to snatch them from the fire of destruction.

The letter concludes with a beautiful doxology, praising God for His power, majesty, and authority. Jude acknowledges that it is God who is able to keep His people from stumbling and present them faultless before His presence with great joy.

In summary, the book of Jude serves as a warning against false teachers who distort the true faith and lead people astray. Jude exhorts his readers to remain faithful, contend for the truth, and show mercy to those who have been deceived. Despite the presence of false teachers, Jude affirms the believers' confidence in God's ability to preserve them and bring them into His glorious presence.

Revelation

"Revelation 21:5 – And he who was seated on the throne said, "Behold, I am making all things new." Also he said, "Write this down, for these words are trustworthy and true."

The Book of Revelation, the final book of the New Testament in the Bible, is a prophetic and symbolic work attributed to the apostle John. It consists of a series of visions and messages that provide insights into the future, spiritual warfare, and the ultimate triumph of God's kingdom. Summarizing such a complex and multifaceted book in 500 words or less is a challenging task, but I will provide a brief overview:

The Book of Revelation begins with an introduction, where John, exiled to the island of Patmos, receives a revelation from Jesus Christ. He is instructed to write down what he sees and send it to the seven churches in Asia Minor. John then experiences a series of vivid visions, including the glorified appearance of Jesus, who reveals himself as the Alpha and the Omega.

The main part of the book describes a series of events that will unfold in the future. John witnesses the opening of seven seals, each revealing different aspects of God's plan for the world. This includes wars, natural disasters, and the rise of false prophets and persecutions. The seventh seal introduces seven trumpet judgments, which bring further devastation to the earth. The final trumpet sounds, leading to the pouring out of seven bowls of God's wrath upon the wicked.

Throughout these visions, there is a constant theme of spiritual warfare between God and Satan, symbolized by various beasts and dragons. The dragon, identified as Satan, seeks to deceive and destroy God's people.

However, John also sees a multitude of believers, representing the faithful, who overcome through their faith in Jesus.

In the later chapters of Revelation, John witnesses the fall of Babylon, a symbol of worldly power and corruption. This is followed by the return of Jesus Christ, described in majestic and apocalyptic language. Jesus defeats the forces of evil, casting Satan into the abyss, and establishes a new heaven and earth. The faithful are rewarded with eternal life in the presence of God, while the wicked face judgment and eternal separation from God.

The Book of Revelation concludes with a vision of the New Jerusalem, a glorious city that represents the redeemed community of believers. In this city, there will be no more pain, sorrow, or death, and God will dwell with His people.

While the Book of Revelation contains intricate symbolism and prophecy, its overarching message is one of hope and encouragement for believers. It assures them that despite the trials and tribulations they may face, God is ultimately in control, and His kingdom will prevail. It calls for faithfulness, perseverance, and a steadfast trust in Jesus Christ, who is portrayed as the victorious ruler over all creation.

The Apocrypha

The Apocrypha refers to a collection of ancient texts that are considered non-canonical by most Protestant Christians but are recognized as part of the biblical canon by some Eastern Orthodox, Oriental Orthodox, and Catholic traditions. This diverse group of writings is often included as an appendix or an inter-testamental section between the Old and New Testaments in these traditions. While the Apocrypha encompasses a range of works, this summary will provide an overview of its significant components.

The Apocrypha includes several books that are not found in the Hebrew Bible, such as Tobit, Judith, Wisdom of Solomon, Sirach (Ecclesiasticus), Baruch, and First and Second Maccabees. These books offer historical accounts, wisdom literature, and moral teachings that shed light on the period between the Old and New Testaments. They cover various themes, including prayer, piety, suffering, faithfulness, and the struggle against oppression.

Tobit narrates the story of a righteous man named Tobit, who endures various trials but remains faithful to God. It also recounts the adventures of Tobit's son, Tobias, and his encounters with angels. Judith tells the tale of a courageous widow named Judith who saves her people by beheading the enemy, General Holofernes. Both Tobit and Judith emphasize the importance of trust in God and the rewards of righteousness.

The Wisdom of Solomon is a collection of philosophical reflections on wisdom, righteousness, and the immortality of the soul. It delves into the nature of God's wisdom and the consequences of both righteous and unrighteous actions. Sirach, written by Jesus ben Sirach, provides practical wisdom for everyday life, covering topics such as friendship, family, wealth, and religious devotion.

The book of Baruch includes prayers and a historical account related to the Babylonian exile. It emphasizes repentance and the hope of restoration for God's people. First and second, Maccabees recounts the struggles of the Jewish people against Hellenistic oppression and the subsequent establishment of the Hasmonean dynasty. These books highlight the importance of religious freedom, fidelity to Jewish customs, and the defense of one's faith.

In addition to these major works, the Apocrypha also contains additional sections and fragments added to certain biblical books, such as additions to the books of Esther and Daniel. These additions provide further details, prayers, and moral lessons related to the original texts.

While the Apocrypha holds religious and historical significance for certain Christian traditions, its canonicity has been a subject of debate. Protestant Christianity generally excludes these texts from the biblical canon, considering them valuable for historical study but not authoritative for doctrine. On the other hand, Eastern Orthodox, Oriental Orthodox, and Catholic churches view them as inspiration and include them as part of their Scripture.

In summary, the Apocrypha is a collection of ancient texts that explore a range of themes, including history, wisdom, and religious devotion. These writings provide valuable insights into the inter-testamental period and offer moral teachings for believers. While their canonicity remains a matter of disagreement among Christian traditions, the Apocrypha continues to be studied and appreciated for its historical, literary, and theological contributions.

Tobit

The Book of Tobit is a biblical narrative that appears in the Old Testament, specifically in the Deuterocanonical books, which are accepted by some Christian denominations but not by others. It tells the story of Tobit, a righteous Israelite living in Nineveh during the Assyrian captivity. Here is a summary of the book:

Tobit, a devout and pious man, was taken into captivity by the Assyrians during the reign of Shalmaneser. He faithfully followed the Jewish laws and customs, even in exile. Despite his righteousness, he faced many trials, including blindness. Tobit became blind and, feeling burdened, he prayed for death. At the same time, in Media, a young woman named Sarah also prayed for death due to the suffering caused by a demon who killed her seven husbands on their wedding nights.

God heard the prayers of both Tobit and Sarah and sent the angel Raphael to assist them. Disguised as a human, Raphael accompanied Tobit's son, Tobias, on a journey to collect a debt. Along the way, Raphael revealed his true identity to Tobias and instructed him on how to use a fish's gall and liver to drive away the demon that plagued Sarah. Tobias followed the instructions, and upon meeting Sarah, he successfully drove away the demon.

Overjoyed with the outcome, Tobias asked for Sarah's hand in marriage. Her father, Raguel, agreed, and Tobias and Sarah were married. During the wedding feast, Tobit, who had remained behind in Nineveh, was anxiously awaiting his son's return. Meanwhile, Raphael instructed Tobias to collect some of the fish's gall to heal Tobit's blindness.

When Tobias and Sarah returned to Nineveh, Raphael applied the fish's gall to Tobit's eyes, and his sight was miraculously restored. Filled with gratitude, Tobit and Tobias praised God. Raphael then revealed his identity as an angel and departed, leaving the family in awe of God's blessings.

After the miracle, Tobit counseled his son to care for his mother and to be charitable. Tobit eventually died at a ripe old age, leaving an inheritance for Tobias and his family. Tobias, in obedience to his father's final wish, accompanied by his wife and son, returned to Media, their ancestral home.

The Book of Tobit concludes with Tobias giving a farewell to his father-in-law, Raguel, and thanking him for the love and care shown to him and his family. He then provides a detailed account of Tobit's righteousness and the miraculous events they experienced. Tobias urges his readers to fear God, praise His name, and trust in Him.

In summary, the Book of Tobit tells the story of Tobit and his son Tobias, who encounter various trials but is ultimately blessed by God's intervention. It emphasizes the importance of faith, obedience, and trust in God's providence. The book also highlights the role of angels in carrying out God's will and the power of prayer in overcoming adversity.

Judith

The Book of Judith is a biblical narrative found in the Old Testament Apocrypha. It tells the story of a brave and cunning Jewish widow named Judith who plays a pivotal role in delivering her people from the oppression of the Assyrian army.

The story is set during the time of the Assyrian conquests when the Israelite city of Bethulia is under siege. The Assyrian general Holofernes leads his mighty army against the city, cutting off its water supply and subjecting the inhabitants to starvation. Faced with imminent destruction, the people of Bethulia, led by their elders, decide to surrender to the Assyrians if relief doesn't arrive within five days.

Judith, a virtuous and devout widow, hears about the city's plight and determines to take action. She puts on sackcloth, fasting and praying for strength and guidance. She hatches a daring plan to deceive Holofernes and bring salvation to her people. Judith prepares herself for a dangerous mission, putting her faith in God and relying on her beauty and intelligence.

She travels to the Assyrian camp accompanied by her loyal maid. Her captivating beauty catches the attention of Holofernes, who invites her to a banquet. Judith presents herself as a defector from the Israelites and gains the general's trust. She beguiles him with her charm, captivating him to the point of intoxication. Seizing the opportunity, Judith severs Holofernes' head while he sleeps and smuggles it out of the camp in her maid's food bag.

With the head of Holofernes as proof of his demise, Judith returns triumphantly to Bethulia. The Israelites are filled with renewed hope and rally against the Assyrians, attacking them with great fervor. The Assyrians, now leaderless and demoralized, retreat in disarray. The city is saved, and Judith is hailed as a heroine.

The Book of Judith highlights the power of faith, courage, and resourcefulness. Judith's unwavering faith in God's guidance, coupled with her quick thinking and determination, enables her to outwit and defeat the powerful enemy. Her actions embody the belief that God can use individuals, even ordinary ones, to accomplish extraordinary things.

The book concludes with a hymn of praise and thanksgiving, celebrating Judith's bravery and the deliverance of the Israelites. It emphasizes the role of divine intervention in their victory, acknowledging that it was God who ultimately protected and saved His people from destruction.

Overall, the Book of Judith serves as an inspirational tale of a strong and fearless woman who rises against adversity to become an instrument of deliverance. It emphasizes the importance of unwavering faith, resourcefulness, and the belief that even the most daunting challenges can be overcome with God's help.

Wisdom

The Book of Wisdom, also known as the Wisdom of Solomon, is a book found in the Septuagint and the Catholic and Orthodox Christian canons of the Bible. It is attributed to King Solomon, who was renowned for his wisdom in biblical tradition. The book consists of philosophical and moral teachings that emphasize the pursuit of wisdom and the rewards of righteous living.

The Book of Wisdom begins with a call to wisdom, portraying it as a divine gift and a source of understanding and virtue. It highlights the benefits of seeking knowledge and warns against the allure of worldly desires and pleasures that lead to destruction. Wisdom is personified as a woman who guides and protects those who embrace her teachings.

The author reflects on the nature of wisdom, describing it as a treasure more valuable than any earthly possession. Wisdom is portrayed as eternal and transcendent, existing before the creation of the world. It is presented as a divine attribute and a reflection of God's nature. The righteous are encouraged to seek wisdom diligently, as it leads to a deeper understanding of God's plan and purpose.

The book also explores the contrast between wisdom and folly. Folly represents ignorance, arrogance, and the rejection of divine guidance. The author emphasizes that wisdom brings knowledge, righteousness, and discernment, while folly leads to ignorance, wickedness, and spiritual blindness. The consequences of choosing folly are highlighted, including the loss of divine favor and the ultimate judgment of God.

The author addresses the theme of immortality, discussing the fate of the righteous and the wicked in the afterlife. The righteous are depicted as being under the special care and protection of God. They are assured of eternal life and peace, while the wicked face divine judgment and punishment. The concept of divine justice is emphasized, with the author affirming that God will reward each person according to their deeds.

Throughout the book, the author emphasizes the importance of righteousness and virtue. The righteous are called to live in accordance with God's laws and commandments, treating others with compassion, justice, and integrity. The pursuit of wisdom is presented as the path to righteousness, leading to a life of moral excellence and spiritual fulfillment.

In summary, the Book of Wisdom is a philosophical and moral work attributed to King Solomon. It emphasizes the pursuit of wisdom as a divine gift and the key to righteous living. The book explores the contrast between wisdom and folly, highlights the consequences of one's choices, and addresses the themes of immortality and divine justice. Ultimately, it encourages the reader to seek wisdom, embrace righteousness, and live a life guided by moral and ethical principles.

Sirach

The Book of Sirach, also known as Ecclesiasticus, is a wisdom book found in the Old Testament Apocrypha. It was written by Jesus Ben Sira, a Jewish scribe who lived in Jerusalem around the 2nd century BCE. The book consists of various proverbs, teachings, and advice on a wide range of topics, offering practical wisdom for living a righteous and fulfilling life.

Sirach begins by praising wisdom as the source of all good things and encourages the reader to seek wisdom diligently. He emphasizes the importance of observing the commandments and living in accordance with God's will. Sirach guides various aspects of life, including the importance of honoring parents, the value of friendship, and the dangers of pride and arrogance.

The book discusses the nature of true wisdom and the consequences of folly. It warns against associating with evil individuals and encourages the reader to choose their companions wisely. Sirach also emphasizes the importance of honesty, integrity, and humility in relationships and dealings with others.

The book provides practical advice on matters such as wealth and poverty, the use of words, and the pursuit of knowledge. Sirach cautions against the love of money and the dangers of excessive ambition. He promotes the idea of contentment and encourages the reader to find joy in the simple blessings of life.

Sirach also reflects on the fleeting nature of human existence, urging the reader to be mindful of the brevity of life and the certainty of death. He encourages a virtuous and righteous life, emphasizing the rewards of righteousness and the consequences of wickedness.

The book contains reflections on the importance of religious devotion, including the value of prayer, fasting, and charitable acts. Sirach stresses the significance of honoring God and the rewards that come from a faithful and devout life.

In addition, Sirach explores various social and ethical issues, such as the treatment of the poor, the proper conduct of rulers, and the responsibilities of children toward their parents. He advocates for justice, fairness, and compassion in society.

Throughout the book, Sirach draws upon the wisdom of earlier Jewish traditions, citing examples from the lives of biblical figures and historical events. He weaves together his teachings with stories and anecdotes to illustrate his points and provide practical guidance for daily life.

In summary, the Book of Sirach offers a comprehensive collection of practical wisdom for living a righteous and fulfilling life. It covers a wide range of topics and guides on matters of personal conduct, relationships, societal ethics, and religious devotion. Sirach encourages the reader to seek wisdom, live in accordance with God's will, and find joy and contentment in a virtuous life.

Baruch

The Book of Baruch is a part of the Old Testament Apocrypha, which is not included in the Hebrew Bible but is found in some Christian canons. It is attributed to Baruch, the secretary and disciple of the prophet Jeremiah. The book contains a series of prayers, hymns, and wisdom literature, primarily addressing the Jewish exiles in Babylon during the sixth century BCE. Below is a summary of the Book of Baruch:

The book begins by setting the historical context, stating that it was written during the Babylonian exile after Jerusalem was conquered and destroyed by the Babylonians. Baruch, the scribe and close associate of Jeremiah, addresses the Jewish people, reminding them of their past disobedience to God's commandments, which led to their current predicament.

Baruch urges the exiles to seek repentance and return to God. He expresses grief and acknowledges the just punishment they are facing due to their sins. Baruch encourages the people to turn away from idolatry and embrace God's law, emphasizing that true wisdom and understanding come from observing God's commandments.

The book then shifts to a reflection on the nature of wisdom. Baruch extols the virtues of divine wisdom, contrasting them with the futility of human pursuits and the emptiness of idols. He encourages people to seek wisdom and understanding, for they are the path to true happiness and the favor of God.

Baruch then offers a prayer on behalf of the exiles, confessing their sins and acknowledging God's righteousness. He pleads for mercy and restoration, asking God to forgive the people and bring them back to their homeland.

Baruch appeals to God's covenant promises and expresses hope in God's faithfulness.

In the later part of the book, Baruch shifts his focus to Jerusalem, personifying the city as a mourning widow. He laments the destruction of Jerusalem, describing it as a consequence of the people's disobedience. Baruch speaks of the restoration of Jerusalem, envisioning a future time when the city will be rebuilt and its inhabitants will return with joy.

The book concludes with a message of hope and comfort. Baruch encourages the exiles to persevere in their faith and trust in God's promises. He assures them that God will eventually deliver them from their captivity and gather them from the nations. Baruch emphasizes that God's mercy and forgiveness are available to those who repent and turn to Him.

Overall, the Book of Baruch serves as a call to repentance, a reflection on the consequences of sin, and a message of hope in God's faithfulness. It reminds the exiles of the importance of obedience, wisdom, and trust in God and offers comfort by assuring them of restoration and redemption.

1 Maccabees

The Book of 1 Maccabees is a historical account that chronicles the events surrounding the Maccabean Revolt in the second century BCE. Here is a summary of the book in 500 words or less:

1 Maccabees begins with a brief background of the political and cultural landscape of the time. The Greek Empire, under the rule of Alexander the Great, had fragmented after his death, and the Seleucid Empire emerged as the dominant power in the region, including Judea. Antiochus IV Epiphanes became the ruler of the Seleucid Empire and imposed Hellenistic practices upon the Jewish people, causing great turmoil and religious oppression.

The book then focuses on the story of Mattathias, a Jewish priest who refused to obey the king's decrees. When an official tried to enforce the Hellenistic practices in Mattathias' village, he killed the Jew who was about to offer a pagan sacrifice and started a rebellion. Mattathias and his sons, known as the Maccabees, fled to the wilderness, where they gathered a loyal following of Jews who were also opposed to the Greek influence.

After Mattathias' death, his son Judas Maccabeus took the leadership role. Judas and his forces engaged in guerrilla warfare against the powerful Seleucid army, achieving several victories despite being outnumbered and outgunned. They destroyed pagan altars, cleansed the desecrated Temple in Jerusalem, and rededicated it to the worship of the God of Israel. This event is commemorated in the festival of Hanukkah.

Judas' military successes drew the attention of the Seleucid king, Antiochus IV. In response, the king sent a larger army to suppress the rebellion. The Maccabees faced overwhelming odds, but through their determination and faith, they achieved remarkable victories, including defeating the Seleucid forces led by Nicanor and Gorgias.

After many battles and political maneuverings, the Maccabees established an independent Jewish state, free from Seleucid control. They established the Hasmonean dynasty, with Simon Maccabeus becoming the high priest and ruler of Judea. Simon and his descendants governed the region for several decades, maintaining a level of autonomy for the Jewish people.

The book concludes with the assassination of Simon Maccabeus and the subsequent rule of his son, John Hyrcanus. While the Maccabean Revolt initially aimed to preserve Jewish religious practices and independence, the Hasmonean dynasty faced internal strife and eventually aligned themselves with the Hellenistic practices they once opposed.

The Book of 1 Maccabees provides a historical account of a critical period in Jewish history, highlighting the resilience and determination of the Maccabees to preserve their faith and culture against significant odds. It serves as an important record of the struggle for religious freedom and the establishment of an independent Jewish state during a time of Greek dominance in the region.

2 Maccabees

The Book of 2 Maccabees is an ancient Jewish text that recounts historical events during the period of the Maccabean revolt against the Seleucid Empire in the 2nd century BCE. Here is a summary of the book in 500 words or less:

2 Maccabees begins with a letter addressed to the Jewish community in Egypt, offering a condensed version of a longer historical account. The book aims to provide a comprehensive narrative of the events surrounding the Maccabean revolt and the subsequent purification and rededication of the Jerusalem Temple.

The book starts by describing the reign of King Antiochus IV Epiphanes, who ascended to the Seleucid throne. Antiochus sought to impose Hellenistic culture and religion on the Jewish people, leading to widespread oppression and persecution. He desecrated the Temple, prohibited Jewish religious practices, and enforced the worship of Greek gods.

A Jewish priest named Mattathias and his five sons, led by Judas Maccabeus, resisted Antiochus' decree. They launched a revolt against the Seleucid forces, engaging in guerrilla warfare tactics and winning several battles against larger armies. The Maccabees fought to defend their religious freedom and the worship of the God of Israel.

Judas Maccabeus and his brothers eventually succeeded in liberating Jerusalem and purifying the Temple. They removed the pagan idols, rebuilt the altar, and reestablished the proper rituals and sacrifices. The rededication of the Temple is celebrated annually as the festival of Hanukkah.

The book also recounts various other military campaigns led by Judas Maccabeus and his brothers against neighboring enemies who sought to exploit political instability. Judas expanded Judea's influence and autonomy, forming alliances with neighboring nations.

During this time, news of the death of Antiochus and the succession of his more tolerant son, Antiochus V, reached Judea. However, the Seleucid Empire was still divided, with rival claimants to the throne. These political changes had mixed implications for the Jewish people, as some rulers continued to support their religious freedom while others sought to suppress it.

The book provides detailed accounts of battles, military strategies, and the heroic deeds of Judas Maccabeus. It emphasizes the importance of faith in God and the defense of Jewish religious traditions. It also highlights the significance of prayer, sacrifice, and remembrance of the ancestors.

Towards the end of the book, several episodes recount the author's beliefs in the efficacy of prayers and sacrifices for the deceased. The author encourages the practice of offering prayers and sacrifices on behalf of the fallen soldiers, expressing the belief in an afterlife and the resurrection of the dead.

In conclusion, 2 Maccabees is a historical narrative that chronicles the Maccabean revolt, the liberation of Jerusalem, and the rededication of the Temple. It highlights the importance of faith, religious freedom, and the defense of Jewish traditions. The book also touches on political changes in the Seleucid Empire and promotes the belief in the efficacy of prayers and sacrifices for the deceased.

Dead Sea Scrolls

The Dead Sea Scrolls are a collection of ancient Jewish texts that were discovered between 1947 and 1956 in the vicinity of the Dead Sea, near the modern-day West Bank. These scrolls are considered one of the most important archaeological discoveries of the 20th century and have significantly impacted our understanding of Judaism and the history of the biblical period.

The scrolls consist of thousands of fragments, comprising both biblical and non-biblical texts, and they are written in Hebrew, Aramaic, and Greek. The majority of the texts date back to the Second Temple period, which spans from the 5th century BCE to the 1st century CE.

Among the Dead Sea Scrolls, the most well-known are the biblical manuscripts. These include fragments of every book in the Hebrew Bible, except for the book of Esther. The biblical texts provide valuable insights into the transmission and preservation of the Old Testament, revealing minor textual variations and confirming the accuracy of the biblical text over time.

In addition to the biblical manuscripts, the Dead Sea Scrolls contain numerous non-biblical texts, offering a glimpse into the religious beliefs, practices, and community life of a Jewish sect called the Essenes, who likely authored and preserved these scrolls. The Essenes were a strict and ascetic Jewish group that lived a communal lifestyle in the vicinity of the Dead Sea during the Second Temple period.

The non-biblical texts include religious writings, legal documents, apocalyptic literature, hymns, prayers, commentaries, and sectarian texts. One of the most significant non-biblical scrolls is the "War Scroll," which describes an apocalyptic battle between the forces of good and evil. Another prominent scroll is the "Community Rule," which outlines the rules and practices of the Essene community.

The Dead Sea Scrolls shed light on the diverse religious and theological beliefs that existed in ancient Judaism. They demonstrate the presence of multiple Jewish sects and highlight the unique perspectives and interpretations of scripture held by different groups.

Furthermore, the scrolls provide important historical information about the social, political, and cultural context of the Second Temple period. They offer insights into topics such as Jewish sectarianism, messianic expectations, priestly rituals, purity practices, and the broader Jewish world at the time.

Since their discovery, the Dead Sea Scrolls have undergone extensive study and analysis by scholars. Their significance extends beyond the academic realm, as they have enriched our understanding of the development of Judaism, the origins of Christianity, and the historical background of the Bible.

In summary, the Dead Sea Scrolls are a collection of ancient Jewish texts discovered near the Dead Sea, comprising biblical and non-biblical manuscripts. They provide valuable insights into the biblical period, the development of Judaism, and the beliefs and practices of the Essene community. These scrolls have had a profound impact on biblical studies and our understanding of ancient Jewish history and theology.

Made in the USA
Coppell, TX
12 March 2024

30037932R00098